Escaping the Lion and the Leopard

by Ellie Porte Parker

*based on the true story of a woman's journey from upheaval and
political change in Africa to life in the United States*

First published by Dog Ear Publishing
4011 Vincennes Rd
Indianapolis, IN 46268
www.dogearpublishing.net

ISBN: 978-1-4575-5181-9

This book is printed on acid-free paper.

While this book is based on a true story, some characters have combined and names have been changed where appropriate

Printed in the United States of America

To Ghabriela Donnelly who lived this story,

to Betty Gallagher who introduced this story to me,

and to our families who supported us and encouraged the project.

Author's Note

The first time I met Ghabriela, she told me, "It is a miracle that I'm here, a miracle that I'm alive. God must want me here for some reason." Then she leaned in and said quietly, "Honey, you can't believe the things I've been through. I can't believe them myself. You know, in Ethiopia, there's a story about the lion and the leopard that I used to hear when I was a small child. The story goes that you see a lion and you run away from it, as fast as you can, and you find the first tree you see and run up it for shelter. You are so happy you find that tree, you don't see the leopard on top and it jumps on you and eats you up in one bite." She sat back and sighed, "Sometimes there are just no good choices — you do whatever you got to do to survive. The story of the lion and the leopard – that's the story of my life."

I was introduced to Ghabriela Donnelly by our mutual friend Betty Gallagher, who thought Ghabriela had a great story, and that I was the one to tell it. I began meeting with Ghabriela and heard her stories of life in Africa and later in the United States. She was born in the late 1940s in a part of Ethiopia very near Eritrea. In 1961 Eritreans began a thirty year fight for independence from Ethiopia that lasted until 1991. During this time an estimated 665,000 Eritrean refugees fled to neighboring Sudan. Ghabriela lived the early part of her life in this area, and grew up in an orphanage there. She finally left Eritrea to come to the United States in 1972 and later returned just long enough to adopt two babies who were caught in that long, long war.

Over the course of about a year of meeting with Ghabriela she told me what had happened in her life. Ghabriela was in her sixties when I met her, and she was a beautiful woman still. She had an engaging smile and wore hand-made beaded jewelry and colorful scarves. She would come over to my house, often bringing wonderful Ethiopian foods she had made herself. We laughed and cried together over the stories she told me. Although all the major events in this story really happened to her, the details and the conversations were often lost long ago. This book is based on her life, but some characters have been combined and incidents have been modified. I took the stories she told me and made them into a first person narrative. What I have tried to do is to preserve the feelings accurately, to share the experience of being completely alone in the world, and to explore how someone can hang on to hope in a situation that appears utterly hopeless. We both hope that the fact that she was able to survive the events in her life, without giving up her soul, will give others in terrible situations something to hold onto, and perhaps make a difference.

Ghabriela told me, "I want people to know about my story, tell about my life. Maybe it will help someone. I didn't tell nobody anything about that part of my life, the part before I became a respectable middle class lady living in the suburbs. Oh, people know I was born in Ethiopia, but it doesn't mean anything to them. I especially want my daughters to know the truth about my life."

Ghabriela's daughters, who are grown now, were adopted from Eritrea when they were babies.

"They were so little when they left there, they don't know about the hunger, the wars. And they don't know nothing about my life before I raised them. They don't know what it is like to have to do things you don't feel good about just to survive. They don't know what it is like to have no good choices in front of you," Ghabriela said.

When I asked her what got her through the very difficult times of her life, Ghabriela told me, "Honey, I learned young, that even when I didn't have much, I got two special things. I got stories and I got dreams. They carried me through, that's for sure."

Although for a long time Ghabriela had wanted to separate herself from her past, she eventually had to find a way to make peace with it. This is really the story of how that happened and how adopting her children from Eritrea gave her that chance. She came to understand that although she had reinvented herself, she had to find a way to incorporate her past life and history into her new life. I think that telling her story enabled Ghabriela to understand it in context and I hope it gave her a greater sense of peace.

Ghabriela and I both want to thank our friend Betty for bringing us together.

CHAPTER

1

I learn it's no use to tell everyone everything you know. They don't understand it anyway. No one here, in my little town of Saratoga Springs, ever think about my past, about the things I been through. Probably wouldn't believe them anyway. I just blend into my life here, try not to stand out too much. So when Mrs. Kay, who was at my house making notes for our adoption home study, take another sip of the nice black coffee I prepared, and ask, "So dear, how did you happen to come here from Ethiopia?" I just add a little coffee to her cup, just to keep it nice and warm, and say, "Oh you know, I met my husband at the USO, and well, that was that." Then I give a little wave to my hand so she'll know it's not too interesting and I can talk about something else.

"Here, Honey," I say to her, "try some of this." Then I give her a piece of special fresh bread I made myself.

The things I been through aren't the things you talk about over a cup of coffee. The things I know about people, the good and the bad, they all with me. Take a long time for me to get where I am, to understand what's important. But I don't tell our social worker, Mrs. Kay, all that then. I keep it inside me. I make up a nice little story about meeting my husband, falling in love, coming to America. It's what she want to hear, I know. After all, we all been growing up on Cinderella.

I want to be a nice middle class lady living with my family in the suburbs. I come here in 1972 and I keep my story hidden. It's not until years later, way after I adopt my babies in 1985 and get them away from Africa, and raise them up, and watch them turn into real American girls who don't have a clue about my life that I think I want to tell my real story. I think I decide to tell it the day they whine they don't have the right designer sneakers. I feel like saying to them be glad you have any sneakers. Actually, I think, be glad you have feet. Be glad you're alive. But I don't say that. They maybe sixteen or seventeen years old by then.

My story start way back in a little village near Tagrid in Ethiopia. Even now when I think back on my life, I try to figure out how I got from there to where I am now. I also think about how I went from being a favorite child, a child doted on and hugged by my mother, to a child all the women in the family think is a burden. Those women were only too happy to give me away to the next relative, the next place.

Life was hard in the village where I was born, even then, before the real troubles came, before famine and war and illness. It was a small village, sitting all by itself in the mountains. You need to cross streams to get there, take a donkey up a hill. In the rural countryside there was nothing but dust and hardworking people. So people live close together, know each other and they don't say anything to start a fuss. They know they all got to get along together for a very long time. They live together this way, years and years, and they know this one was that one's granddaughter, they know who cheated who, who helped who, like that. They are like a big family. Life for everyone is tough, work from sunup to sundown, think all the time about the crops, the weather, try to coax the ground into giving up a little food. But still, children are welcomed, families are close, and people take care of each other.

The priests visit the families regular, so everyone knew what was right to do. The old men in the village spend hours praying in the village square, and the women ask the family priest for advice every hour it seem like. Religion is a part of everything. People wake up and pray, they talk to God, and they leave things in God's hands. It make it easier that way, because you don't have to plan too much yourself. But when you do something against the rules, people feel it in their hearts. They take it serious.

And that's where my story take a turn. My birth is a scandal, turns out. You see, my father left my mother years before I was born, and only come back long enough to get her pregnant, and then he up and die. In that village, in the late 1940s, what my father did was considered the worst thing any man could do. He left. Men could get away with a lot, but not that. They could be lazy, they could cheat, but in that village, no one forgive leaving. He just up and went away, leave my mother and all the children they had together to fend for themselves. My parents were married long, long time when my father wander off.

Who knows why he did it. Maybe he just lose interest, maybe he see some young girl and fall in love. He wouldn't be the first man ever to wander off, but you can still imagine how people talk. Their tongues never stop wagging for weeks. The church throw him out, the church ladies cluck their tongues, the family priest come and visit my mother, hold her hand, give her sympathy. I am sure of it.

I don't know if my mother forgive him or not, but from everything I been told, she still love him, carry him in her heart. But, my mother, she do what she need to get on with life. She care for the children she had who survive, bury the

ones who didn't, and fit herself into the village as best she can.
No one there is a stranger to hard work. Three healthy children she raise by the time I was even born. The girls, named
Lula and Gelila, had grown up, married, and had families of
their own. Lula stay close to my mother in our village, and
Gelila move away to the beautiful town of Asmara. Only the
youngest, a boy, stay home. His name was Andu, and he was
a special gift to her, kind, handsome, hardworking.

So there was my mother, forty years old, only Andu still
at home, when my wandering father come back into her life
after being gone for years. Just show up one day, from the way
I heard it. Despite all he had put her through, despite the dis-
grace, she take him back. She love him still; she never stop loving him. And they were still married, after all. In that village
people don't divorce no matter what anyone do.

She get pregnant, and then he die, just when she thought
he'd be there forever. He died before I was even born. My
mother was happy to have me, but from what I overhear in
whispers while I was growing up, not everyone in the family
feel that way. I start to understand very young that my sisters
hold bitterness in their hearts for him. My two older sisters
were already grown up when I was born. Women in Ethiopia
marry young. Eleven, twelve, thirteen is not unusual age to
marry back then. But they come back once in a while to visit
and I remember hearing them talk.

"She look just like him too," Gelila whisper, "dark like
him, and with his smile."

Lula shakes her head. "Mamma just never stood up to
that man. He own her heart."

Gelila sighs. They shake their heads with disapproval.

And to make things worse, I was my mother's favorite.
She play with me, spoil me. I cannot remember her exactly,
but to this day, I can remember the feelings, the feelings of

being a child someone love, someone want. Maybe it is those feelings I have been searching to find again my whole life. I think those feelings stay in me, make me who I am.

But it don't matter anyway. I know what it was like to be loved, to have that power in my heart. I have only to smile, and my mother's face lights up. I feel her arms hold me in a hug; she keep me safe. And her smell, like herbs and musk, stays with me. I have only to whimper, and she is there. She protects me.

I don't know anger in my heart at that time. She protects me from everything. We are joined at the hip. She raise an eyebrow, give me a look, and I do what I can to please her. And I feel that love with me all the time.

But then, everything change fast, in an instant, when I am three years old, maybe four. I don't know a thing about what is going on. No one tell me anything. But I know something is very wrong. I don't see my mother, she isn't there beside me when I wake up and isn't there to feed me my breakfast. I don't remember that time very well, don't remember her being sick or nothing. But I remember all of a sudden seeing lots of people in the house. And I remember the faces. One look at those faces and you know something is wrong. One look at those faces and your heart just twists up.

I remember Andu keeping me away from the bedroom, and I just get a little peek at what's going on in there. I see ladies wrap cloth up around my mother. I will find out that my mother has died. But at first, I don't know what happen, no one talk to me about it. We don't have funeral homes in Tagrid and we don't let the body sit around very long. It's a hot climate and it wouldn't work out so good to do that. The idea is to bury the body sun up to sun up. So things happen fast. I see people weep; I see them wring their hands. It scares me, and for the first time in my life, my mother isn't around to make things right. I remember, more than anything, that feeling inside of being scared.

But then, my brother, Andu, come over to me, kneel beside me and hold my hand. He talk softly. I can remember, the whole time, people was wandering around our house, doing things. They put her body in a coffin, closed, like we do there. Then people get together and take the coffin up the hill, to the cemetery. But you know, at that time, even though I see the coffin, and I know my mother is in it, I still I think my mother is going to wake up, to come back to me. I think this for a long time.

The crying, the casket, the church on the hill just all blur together. But my brother, I remember. And I remember how Andu take me home after the funeral, how he hold my hand. At first, the family crowd around. Everyone come in, there was food everywhere. Oh, I'll tell you, poor as we were, there was some good food there. The neighbors made up special foods. I remember the smells more than anything. Oh those wonderful smells, full of warmth and spice, they just fill the air. I stand at the table, running my fingers along the edge of the wood, looking at all the bowls with steam curling up, carrying all that smell of food right to my nose. I shift from foot to foot, thinking how my mother should be along to ask me if I want something, to coax me, to twist off a bit of something and pop it in my mouth with a smile. But she isn't here, isn't anywhere. I feel scared, but still, I reach over to one of the bowls and twist off a bit of something for myself. I know in that second nothing will ever be the same.

People are still just sort of visiting, and setting up even more food, and wandering around. "What will happen to that little one?" I hear people ask one another. I see shrugs.

"No one will want that homely little thing," I hear one of the women whisper. I am shocked. They mean me, I think. Until that moment, I always feel beautiful.

Andu sees my look, and he pulls me toward him. "Don't worry, Ghabriela, I will take care of you. I won't let anything happen," he whispers. Even though I only remember that time in little pieces, bits here and there, I can still remember just how Andu looked. Even as young as he was, he was dignified, and his smile – his smile will light up the moon, I'm telling you. He had such kindness, such goodness inside, it just spilled out for everyone to feel.

Pretty soon everyone leave the house. My sisters go back to their families. The aunts, the uncles, they disappear into their own lives. I remember, pretty soon it's quiet, and there's just me and my brother. Things are less scary when he is there. To me, he seem so big and grown up. But still, he is only in his teens, and he will have a lot to take care of.

That night, I lie in bed and think if I am a very good girl, my mother will come back. But she doesn't. And I can remember, little by little, I'm getting madder and madder. No matter what I do, nothing helps. I never see her again.

CHAPTER

2

But after my mother die, everything change, of course. Andu stay home and take care of me, those first few weeks. But pretty soon, he has to go back to the fields to work. In the rural countryside, only the women take care of the children. The men got other things to do. So he has to think what to do about me. Although I got the two older sisters, older than Andu, with families of their own, I hardly know them. Lula lives close by, but she busy with her family and Gelila live way far away in Asmara. It's so far away, I hardly ever see her. They got their own problems. But Andu love me, and he feel responsible for me.

There he is, a handsome young man, with no mother or father now. My brother always want to stay on the farm, in the country. He feel like this is the place he belong, the place where everyone know him. And he wants to take care of me. He thinks he can make it work. What he needs is a wife, and at fifteen, he's old enough to marry. But he got to marry someone who can help him, someone who can take care of me.

In Tagrid, families arrange marriages for their children when they are very young. It's not formal, not written down, but the families get together when they have children and decide who should marry who. And it work, usually. To understand it, you got to understand what life is like for my family, for the people who farm back then. Family is everything and people marry in their early teens. They are promised to each other from the time they are babies. Long as everyone does their share of the work, husband and wife cooperate, what more do you need? They all come from same place, all know same people, all the families pitch in. And so it has already been arranged for Andu to marry someone.

So Andu decides this is the right time for him to marry. It's all set up; he just goes with it. But oh Lordy, the girl he gets for a wife, she just hate me, and I just hate her. I don't know why we hate each other so much. Even though I feel the love and care from Andu, the minute he leaves the house, go to the fields which he have to go sun up to sun down, I'm alone. The wife, she starts being mean to me. That's what I remember. I don't even remember her name, just the meanness. I try to think sometimes, now that I'm a grown woman, a mother myself, why she was so terrible to me. I guess she really was only a kid herself, fourteen or fifteen, just married, trying to take care of a kid who she don't know, don't care about. Probably that's how it seems to her. But still, she must have had to have a mean streak to act the way she did. Sometimes it wasn't even the way she acted but the way she looked at me, and the way her mouth turned down when she glanced my way, as if I'm something bad in her vision.

And me, I can remember the anger I feel all the time. I'm so angry I can bust open any second. My mamma is not coming back. She gone and I don't know why or how. I'm not anyone's favorite anymore. No one have time to brush my hair, to give me hugs, to giggle with me. If I whimper, no one is there to see what I want, to make sure I have what I need. Now if I whimper, my brother's wife push me, or slap me to shush me up, to stop me from being annoying. And I don't like this. I don't like it at all. So I'm not being my best self either. I do what I can to upset her any chance I get.

So there we are, me and my brother's wife, trapped together all day long, not liking it one bit and both of us thinking of ways to make the other one even more miserable. She never show me love or anything, and I'm always looking for love because with my mom, I was the favorite. When I am with this girl in the daytime, when Andu's not around, she won't give me food. So what I remember the most is being hungry. Once you have been really, really, hungry, you never forget it.

I remember special, one day my brother left for the farm and his wife was up to something, I don't know what. She get kind of dressed up a little, put on some pretty clothes and she want to go somewhere. She just about to leave the house when she see me looking at some stuff left over from breakfast. We don't have no refrigerator or nothing, but there's some food there. It's my favorite that she has wrapped up and set on the table. And I'm just looking at it, like I can taste it on my tongue, and I'm just waiting for her to leave, because I can just imagine it on my tongue, can feel it. She see how I'm looking at it, and she know what I'm gonna do. She put her hands on her hips and say, "Ghabriela, you touch that food, I'm gonna beat you till you can't sit. You hear me, missy?" She always talk to me like that.

I have a mad look on my face and kind of flounce around. I don't care. I don't care if she beat me or not.

"Think you're so smart? You can just stay outside then all day," she say and grab me by the arm, hard enough to really hurt, to leave a mark, and pull me out of the house. She dragging me by now, and I'm kicking and kicking, trying to kick her knee where it really hurts. We got a regular war going, her and me.

She get me out of the house, and lock the door. "You can just stay outside all day, smarty pants," she tell me.

"But I don't have any food, or water," I wail.

"Well, that's just too bad isn't it?" she say, and she leave.

I sit outside by myself in the dust. I'm maybe four years old, maybe five. I'm feeling hungrier and thirstier as each minute goes by. It's hot outside, really hot in Ethiopia during the day. First I just try standing by the fence, digging my foot around a little, day-dreaming. Then I sing a little to myself, like my brother do some-time. But I start to get hungrier and hungrier and thirstier and thirstier and madder and madder. Pretty soon, I remember dig-ging just like dog to get into the house. I'm determined. She locked me out and I'm gonna get in this time. And somehow, some way, I do get inside the house.

I finish all the food on the table. I just keep cramming everything in my mouth until it's all gone. I can't stop myself, it's like I'm a crazy person. She come home and she is scream-ing. She take a broom and break it over my back. I think she gonna kill me one of these times, but I don't care. She tell me I better not say nothing to my brother if I know what's good for me.

That night, I wear sleeves down to my wrists to cover the bruises on my arms. I don't say nothing, I'm just trying to eat so fast. I remember she pinch me under the table, my feet with her feet, she tell me slow down, and the minute she pinch me, I know something she gonna do the minute my brother's not there, so I can get up, and go and sleep. My brother say, "What's the matter, how come you didn't eat?"

I say, "I'm full," and I just go. I don't tell Andu about it. It's a pride thing, I guess. In my village I learned that people try to solve their own problems, they keep things to them-selves, especially bad things. I'm little, but I already know this. I already want to prove I can handle things.

But still there are plenty of days from then on, that she lock me out, don't leave me no food, and I'm hungry. It's what I remember the most, being hungry — maybe that and being angry.

It wasn't too long after that that Andu start to figure out something is not right. One day he say to me, "I want you to come to the farm with me." I felt so happy inside. I can still remember that feeling. I smile for the first time in a long time. When he go to the farm, he always take a lunch pail full of food to eat later. He carry the food with him that day, and it was something that smelled really wonderful. I could smell that food the whole way, and you know, to this day I can remember that smell and how good it made me feel. But even though I am happy for that minute, I don't look like a happy person no more. The way I walk is like a sad person, the way I stand is like a sad person, the whole way my face is — I always look uncomfortable because I have so much inside of me, so much anger, so much hurt. Somehow he knows that. He is only in his teens then, but he sees something was very wrong. He say, "What is troubling you, why are you so sad?"

I couldn't answer. It had been a long time since I let my feelings out, even put my feelings into words. I was pushing them back all the time, trying not to think about them, trying to survive, keep quiet. I don't say nothing at first, just look down at the dirt. I don't know exactly how old I was then, and I hadn't gone to school yet, but I was old enough to understand what was happening.

He put his arm around me, squeeze me gently, and ask, in that soft voice of his, "Are you happy here? Is there something going on? I feel there is something, something you are not telling me."

The minute he say that, oh boy, everything come out. I stand there in the field, his lunch box letting out all kinds of good smells, the heat rising from the ground so you could feel it, and tears start running down my face. Somehow, I can't keep anything in at all, all those feelings I'd been pushing back and pushing back just came tumbling out, spilling all over both of us, and I couldn't stop them.

I tell him about how she hit me, how she pinch me, how she lock me out. I tell him how all day long, I don't get nothing to eat, sometimes even nothing to drink. I tell him this happening, that happening. What I don't tell him, but I think he know in his heart, is that that isn't the worst part. It isn't the hitting and the being hungry that hurt the most. It is being with someone, sunset to sundown who don't care about me, who hate me. I want to be loved again, cherished, connected to someone.

But now he knows. Remember, he was still really only a boy. He is married and working all day on a farm just to get food to eat. He is troubled but he is not sure what to do. He asks me, just like I was an adult, "What can I do?" We look at each other.

That day I spend all day on the farm with him, and I can see this problem work on him. He looks tired, move slower than usual, and I don't see him flash that beautiful smile. At the end of the day, he sit with me on a bench and he says, "I've been thinking about this all day. I think you will be better off if you live with one of our sisters. We got two grown up sisters." Then he do something unusual. He give me a choice. It's unusual in Ethiopia, maybe anywhere, to give child as young as I am then a choice, but he does this. To this day, I appreciate that. He say, "You decide, which one you want to live with — Gelila or Lula?"

Gelila I never see, because she live far away, in the city, in Asmara. Lula, I know a little bit. She live in the country like us, and sometimes she come over. So I know that sister. They are both older and are married and have children before I was even born.

I think about this for a while, and finally I say, "I seen Lula, and I know her. I want to go live with Gelila. I never seen her before, except maybe once at the funeral." I don't know if he talked to them about it, how they feel, I don't know nothing. All I know is he give me a choice.

When I think about it now, it's kind of an odd choice that I made. I think most kids would choose the person they knew a little. Plus Lula lived closer by, so I would have seen my brother more often; I would have stayed in the countryside near the people who knew me. Maybe even then, I felt that somehow I was an outcast, I don't know. But anyway I choose something I don't know about at all. I guess I always want to try something new in life. When I think about it, I always do that in my life, try the thing I don't know. You know there's an expression, "The devil you know is better than the devil you don't." But me, I never hear that expression till way later, and I am always thinking something I don't know is better than what I'm living through. I think it's because, deep inside, I believe there's something really good out there. Remember, I was once a loved child and that has made all the difference.

So that's what I choose, the sister I don't know, Gelila. Which again, God willing, I guess that's where God wants me. Otherwise, why would I make that choice? I don't even know the city, the country — I don't know nothing about where I'm going. For me is no different, just the idea is that I haven't seen that one, so I want to see her. So that's how I wound up living with my sister, Gelila. You know what I told you about the lion and the leopard, running from one bad situation to another? I guess that's what happened to me.

CHAPTER

3

My brother has to wait for a while before he can take me there. He has to wait until it's a time he can leave the farm work. And, we have to choose a time when we can cross the river. Some seasons the water is too high to get across. Finally it's the right time for him to bring me to the city. We plan for the trip. He packs my things, which doesn't take much time. And he packs a little knapsack for the trip, with water and food. I look into it and smile. It looks like good things to eat. There is fruit, and as always, *injera*, bread shaped like a pancake. I hope maybe there will be a little candy but I don't expect that and there isn't. He will take me all the way there himself, and I'm happy to spend time with him. This is a long, long trip.

We live in the mountains and we have to walk for a long time, down steep hills at first. I remember the smell of the hot dry dust, the feel of the sand and rocks underneath my feet. Thank God I got some sandals to wear for this trip. Usually I go barefoot. Sometimes we slide, we hear little pebbles pinging down the side of the mountain. Andu holds my hand in his. His hand is cool and dry. Some people ride on donkeys to get down the mountain, but we don't have a donkey. We just walk and walk. Finally we get into a little town at the bottom of the mountain, and there is a little hut there. It's where the bus stops.

People are sitting around crowded in to get some shade. They are fanning themselves with their hands, with straw-like things, with anything they got. There are people with chickens that they hold by the wings, and women with babies that they nurse on their breasts.

Andu and I find a place to sit. I never been on a bus before, or even seen one. It pulls up with a loud noise and lots of black smoke pouring out a pipe in the back. I jump at the noise and everyone laughs. When it pulls up to the stop, Andu tells the bus driver where he is going and the driver lets out a little whistle, like that is a long ride. Then Andu takes out some coins from a little handkerchief that he has wrapped in his pocket and gives them to the bus driver, carefully counting them out. He gently leads me up the step, and we find two seats together. He lets me sit by the window, which is open. The smell from the bus comes pouring in as it takes off, but at least there is some air.

We sit on the bus for hours. It stops every once in a while and people come in, people go out. Sometimes when the bus stops, there is a little store. Then I get to look at the tea and the candies. The candies are all kinds of colors, blues and reds and green. Just like a rainbow. I think how they will taste on my tongue, but I know we don't have money to buy that stuff. Andu open a little sack he is carrying and bring out some water for me, and some *injera*. We sit down on a rock and eat it. I feel happy inside, just to be with Andu, and just to be on this adventure. I don't think what will happen in the future.

We ride for maybe three, four hours. We pass through trees, and riverbeds. Some are cracked and dried up. It's the dry season now. Once, we see some hippos sloshing around in what's left of a mud hole. Mostly we see monkeys. The monkeys listen for the bus to stop and when it does, they come around, looking for food.

After a while, the landscape change, and there are different kinds of trees, more houses. It's beautiful and different. I never see anything like this before in my whole life. Finally the bus driver calls out, "Last Stop" and we get out. We walk some more.

We are in Asmara. There are streets with stores, and beautiful houses painted in all sorts of pretty colors, in pinks and yellows, with pretty flowers. It's so very different from that dry and dusty farm, I could never have even imagine something like this exist in the world. The city sits high above the sea and we pass beautiful places on the way to my sister's house. Later I will understand it is a wealthy area where Europeans vacation, the part of Africa most Americans never even imagine. Later I will run around the streets of Asmara, looking at the beautiful homes, dreaming one day of living the good life, and I'll press my nose against the store windows, plotting on ways to get a sweet. But right then, I am just speechless.

After we get off the bus, we need to walk a couple of miles to my sister's house. It's hot, but I don't even whine that much, because I am so surprised by all the new things I see. And besides, my brother encourage me, speaking softly. When we get to my sister's house, I see it's not fancy like some of the houses we've passed, but it's nice. It has a little garden, and it's painted all pretty. My sister greet us.

I remember that minute. She throw her arms around Andu and hug him. You can tell there is love there. She look at me, and sigh. "And this must be Ghabriela," she say. She look like she's not thrilled, but she say, "Come on in." Three of her kids are behind her and they are looking around her, peeking shyly at me.

There are two boys, Able and Salameh, one about my age, the other, maybe a little younger, and a girl, a few years younger than me, named Genet. First thing I notice, is they so light, they don't look like me, and it surprise me. I don't figure it out at first.

I stand just by the door when I first come into the house. I don't know what I expect, but this isn't it. All my short life I live in one kind of place, the countryside. The houses where I lived were all mud huts. The walls of the huts are shaped to sort of make cabinets, places to hold things, so you don't even need much furniture. And the ground is always dirt and grass. You can see the hills in the distance, covered in green with trees and flowers all the time in Tagrid.

But here, I can see when we came from the bus, everything is different. Even though my sister's house is not big and fancy like some of the houses we passed, it's still very different from what I'm used to. The floor is beautiful brick, not mud like I'm used to. Everywhere you look, things are made of brick, of tile. And there's furniture, too.

And as I stand there and look, I can smell all the wonderful things cooking. But even the smells are different, and I can tell there are lots of foods I've never even thought about coming out of the kitchen. I want to run there and eat everything I can, but I'm trying very hard to be polite. I want to make a good impression.

"Well, Ghabriela," my sister say, "Don't just stand there with your mouth open. Go help the other kids."

I feel a little shocked. I'm used to Andu's voice so kind and gentle, and when I hear this harshness, I jump. I go to help bring things from the kitchen. I help and Genet, the girl younger than me, tries to help too, although she's too little to do much, really. The boys sit and tell jokes and punch each other. It will turn out to be the way things are for years.

The dishes that come from the kitchen are filled with wonderful things, some I already know. My sister has made special company food, including soups, and special breads.

She is thrilled my brother is here and has made all this in his honor. But there are also things I've never seen before, little meatball things and sauces. It turn out my sister's husband was part Italian, and there are lots of people from Italy living in Asmara, and lots of the food is a sort of combination of Ethiopian and Italian. And it is all wonderful.

There are so many Italians in Ethiopia because the Italians had actually made a colony of Eritrea in the late 1800s. A lot of them were involved in all the wars and then somehow or other they stay here and have families here. I don't learn till much later that lots of different countries had their eye on Asmara. One time or another the English, the Turks, the Egyptians were here. And later the Americans came and set up shop to listen in on the rest of the world. So my sister's husband was raised here and his family live in the area. His family hate my sister. I don't know any of this then. I just look at her kids and her house, and I think she have a pretty nice life. My sister's been married, already a long time, since she was fourteen or fifteen, but her husband died recently. She got five kids altogether, two already grown, and then the three living at home. She has a reasonable house and some help with the kids. Her oldest child is off studying to be a nurse. Until her husband died, she was doing pretty good, but now she's in a struggle, fighting with her husband's family, and generally not in a good mood.

At first I get myself a big plate of food and stay near my brother. I'm happy feeling him close, and happy knowing there's plenty to eat. I don't want to think about him going. I push it out of my mind. It's enough that he's here, next to me.

My sister look at my plate of food. I've got lots of everything piled on it. "Gonna have to watch that one," she say, with kind of an edge in her voice.

I look at the ground, dig my foot in a little. I feel like a little chill, like I know in my heart things are not going to work out.

She keep looking at me, and I feel more and more uncomfortable. I want to stay near Andu, but I don't want to be under that stare, so gradual like, I wander off. I kind of want to see the rest of what's in the house, anyway.

I run my fingers along the walls, which are cool and smooth and made of stone. They feel so different than the mud walls I'm used to. I run my fingers along the couches and chairs, too. The furniture is soft and pretty. I'm interested in everything I see. There is so much, I can hardly take it all in. It is like I've been dropped onto another planet.

I wander into the bedroom and the thing I see that really catch my eye is a picture sitting right up there on the dresser. I see a photograph only one time before. This photograph is black and white. It looks like a family picture, something special maybe, and I stand right next to it to see it better. I see my sister and her kids and her husband. Her husband's light, which surprises me. In my village, everyone there looks pretty much alike, and no one there is this light. In Tagrid, they wear the same clothes, talk the same language. Asmara has all kinds of people from all over the world. They look different, dress different, talk different.

I hear footsteps, and I feel my sister's eyes boring into me.

"Ghabriela, next time ask permission before you come into my bedroom. That picture you are looking at is my family. Now why don't you go out and join the other kids?"

She doesn't say anything really mean, but I can tell she doesn't like me. And I know she thinks I'm nosey, going into her room, poking around. I hear her whisper later, "What a strange child."

I find the other kids and we all go outside and kick around a ball for a while. Genet is too young to really play, but I protect her. I keep the boys from chucking the ball her way and hitting her in the head. They wild, I can see that. They do whatever they want and no one say nothing to them. They like little princes.

When we come in my brother tells me that he has to leave early the next morning. It's a very long trip back to Tagrid and he has work to do there.

I get up very early, just so I can say goodbye to him.

He hugs me tight and says softly, "Be a good girl, Ghabriela and be happy here. And remember I love you."

I hug him back and tell him that I don't want him to go. I'm struggling to hold back tears. In my heart I know things will never be the same and somewhere in my brain I feel fear, like something dark just sneaking there.

"I'll be back to visit soon as I can, next year maybe," he tells me. His wife will be having her baby soon and it will be old enough to bring with him next time. He will bring them both and we will celebrate being together again, he says. I'm not too crazy about seeing his wife, but I put that out of my mind. I just think about when Andu will visit again.

4

It don't take long for things to change after my brother leaves. I'm happy at first that there are other kids to play with. The boys are about my age, and I can join in their games. Genet is young enough to feel like a little sister, someone I can look after.

People in the village laugh when they see me with my sister's whole family. Little smiles curl up in the corner of their mouths as they watch us in the candy store, at the grocers, in the winding streets. My sister is trotting around with all her kids and me. She is pretty light and they are even lighter, being half Italian. They look like they could be anything. But me, I'm very dark and I stick out in this crowd. I don't know nothing about this at first. I don't think about it. I look like I always look. But everywhere we go, people poke my sister and laugh. "Where'd you get that one?" they ask.

And I hear people whisper, "Look how dark that one is. Where'd she come from?"

My sister ignores it, and pulls me away by the hand, but I notice after every time it happens, she seem more annoyed with me, and has shorter patience. And other things about me bother her, too. I hear her one time, talking to her best friend. They are sitting in the kitchen having coffee and something, some kind of food. I hear her say, "Every time I see her, I just get cold inside. She look just like my father. Just like him."

I know the way she says it, it isn't a good thing. But I don't know anything about my father, except he left the family for a very long time. Maybe she's angry about that. Who knows? She doesn't say anything to her friend about how dark I am, how I stick out and make her kids stick out. She doesn't have to. But she does say one more thing that interests me. She reach her hand over to her friend's hand and says, "Also, since she came here, Mamma's been visiting me in my dreams."

Her friend looks up, surprised, but only a little. I know her friend been visited by her own Mamma in her own dreams. Wasn't so unusual there for people to get signs, for dead Mamma's to show up in all sorts of dreams.

My sister goes on, "I don't think she's happy with the way I treat Ghabriela. But Lordy, I'm doing my best," my sister says, and then don't say no more about it right then.

Well, visits from Mamma or not, my sister treats me worse and worse as time go by. In the very beginning of my time there, I'm at home and helping take care of Genet and playing with her. I am close to my little sister and we stay home and play and no one bothers us. But pretty soon, I go to a school, like kindergarten. The boys, who are older, are already in regular school.

My sister brings both me and Genet to the church that day and introduce us to the teacher. She push Genet toward her, saying "And this is my daughter Genet."

"And who is this little one?" The teacher asks, looking at me.

I smile up at her. I start to say something about being her cousin, but my sister hush me.

"This is Ghabriela, who I look after," she say, frowning at me, letting me know to be quiet.

The teacher smiles, and introduces us to the other children. I will be staying there for school, but Genet is too young, and she'll be at home with Gelila. The school is run by the church, the Orthodox church, so they teach us a little about religion, a little about playing together, and they read us stories. I like it.

The minute I start going to school, the minute I start going with her outside the family, things change with my sister. She starts treating me like she treats her housekeeper. She don't treat me like one of her kids. I can feel the difference and I don't like this. Then on top of it all, her kids sit down at the table together to have breakfast, lunch or dinner. In the meantime, my sister tells me to go in the other room and to wait until they finish. My eye is right there on that food. I look at their food, and my mouth waters. I smell it and I feel like I can taste it. And they sit together all three of them, her kids that are still home, and they scoop up the food and they giggle and they poke each other. But me, I'm sitting in the other room, looking in.

When they finish, when they don't want no more, I come in with the housekeeper and we eat together. It's nothing like the good food they were eating. It's not the fresh beautiful vegetables and the just baked bread, filling the room with wonderful smells. No, this is the left over stuff, the food no one else wanted.

The housekeeper is a local woman who is cheerful. She just comes in to help out afternoons. My sister isn't a rich lady, but it's common in Eretria to have help if you have kids and have a little extra money. Labor is cheap. The housekeeper is kind enough, but she's busy. She has her own kids to go home to. She tries to keep things upbeat when we eat, but I think she knows it's not right. And besides she can feel my rage, and it upset her. She can see how my body tense up and I know she tries to soothe me, talk extra soft and calm me down. Even when I'm very little, I have a sense about people, I know how they are feeling, even when I don't know how I know.

It seem like I'm angry all the time now. Inside me, this hot thing is growing. I'm feeling something I don't have a name for. I just know this feeling lives with me like a caged animal, snarling, angry, uncoiling itself. That separation from the other children is something I never understand, not then, not now. Even though those are her kids and I'm only her sister, there is something wrong about this. First, we all together, then we are separated. It's in my heart, my brain, my soul. All those years ago, and I can still remember that feeling, that feeling of being treated different. And I can still feel the anger in the pit of my stomach, like something hot living there. I can hardly remember the time when my mother looked at me and smiled just to see me. But I think somewhere inside, I know it's possible to have people feel love for me, and I know I don't have it anymore. I know I've lost something important; I just feel it all the time. I think all my life, I search for this thing.

Things start to go from bad to worse. There's one after-noon that starts things down a really bad road. I come home from school. And when I walk in the door, Gelila tells me she is going to be taking Genet shopping soon, get her some pretty stuff. I wish that I could have nice clothes and those fancy little shoes that shine and have a strap going across, like some of the girls have, but I know there is no use asking.

People in Eritrea are very fashion conscious. It's different than lots of people imagine Africa to be. They get fashions from Europe here, and the people who can afford it buy the best clothes in the world. The people who can't afford the best clothes try to copy stylish clothes, and the rest of us just wish we could and wear what we can scrounge.

I'm in the scrounger category. So I'm not so happy that Genet is the one she's taking shopping, and I'm sure my face show it, but I don't say nothing.

Then Gelila turns to me and tells me I need to do some chore. I always seem to need to do some chore. We heat the house with wood and someone always got to put wood on the fire, and that's one of my regular chores. Someone also needs to wash the floors, and this time, that's what she tells me to do. We had brick floors, really beautiful floors, with a nice drain in the middle, wash everything down. But, oh my, it gets dirty fast. And always she tells me to wash it.

So that day, she says to me, "Wash up the floor." She say it in a sort of nasty voice.

I think to myself, what do I want to do that for? Why should I? But I get out the mop. I just kind of doodle around with it, you know not doing anything.

She put her hands on her hips. "You not doing that right," she say.

Well, I know that. I never do anything right she ask me to do. I deliberately mop the stuff the wrong way, away from the drain.

She is getting more and more annoyed, I can see. So finally she tell me to wash something down. Get the bucket and the soap, she tell me.

I glare at her. I get the water, then I get the soap. Then something happen I can't explain. That hot ball of anger take over. I'm not thinking, I'm not saying to myself, this is right, this is wrong. I'm just acting, just doing. I take the soap and pour it over the furniture, not in the bucket.

She look crazy for a second, her eyes light up, like one of those horror movies I see now in this country. Really. She lose control of herself. She grab the broom and start hitting me with it, smacking it everywhere she can reach.

But I'm not going to let her see me cry. She can do anything to me she want, I don't care. And by this time, she's totally lost, she's not thinking either. She just keep hitting me and hitting me with that broom. I shout, I yell, the whole neighborhood come running. They think like someone is getting killed. She finally break the broom over my back, and start slapping me with her hands, just as the neighbors come in. They drag her off me. They try to calm her down.

Funny thing, I remember just standing in the corner watching, as they all gather around her. There's maybe five or six of them, women from the neighborhood, trying to get her to get a hold of herself. No one pay me any attention. It's like I'm not there. The neighbors already got me pegged as a bad apple and they love my sister. They think she is a saint for taking me in.

My back is stinging, everything hurts, but nothing is broken. But you know, it isn't getting hit that upset me so much. There are worse things than that, and I know them all.

After this, it's like a routine between us. She tell me to do something, I do it as bad as I can, she beat me. I get used to it. I don't care.

I think we both know things aren't right. My sister look upset all the time, and the other kids can feel her anger, and see how she treats me. The boys think it's okay to treat me bad too, because their mother does it. Somehow, if anything goes wrong, it's my fault. But underneath, my sister is unhappy with this situation, with me for sure, but also, I think with herself.

I hear her tell her friend that my Mamma is coming to her more and more frequent in her dreams. Seem like she there every night, she says, worrying about Ghabriela.

"I don't know what to do, I try to be nicer, but she makes me crazy, not myself," I hear my sister say.

Things go along like this for a very long time, right up until Andu's next visit. It should have been a wonderful time because we were all excited about seeing Andu and preparing for his family to visit. He has only come back a couple of times since I been here. On this visit he is bringing his wife and his little daughter, who is a few years old now. We hadn't seen him for a very, very long time. We clean and make special foods.

The afternoon they all coming, Andu and his family, my sister send me to get some stuff for the party, you know for food. She tell me she in a big hurry, I need to get the things as fast as I can.

"Don't you be dawdling, taking forever," she tells me.

I shake my head, I will be good. I'm happy, I love to go buy food. The food there was so good, so fresh, we buy it every day. She would send me to get tomatoes, and to get bread, the flat kind you cooked, fruits all that kind of thing. But in Eritrea when you buy something, the shopkeeper usually gives you a little treat, a candy. They make them out of sugar and caramel and they are sticky and sweet and I can still remember how they taste. I dreamt of them at night, dreamt of them melting in my mouth, of tasting their sweetness.

So when she send me to the store, I'm happy, but I don't buy everything I can at one place. I go to as many stores as I can because I know at each place they will give me a little treat. I get the banana at one store and get a treat, get the mango at another store get another treat, get the peach at another store, another treat, like this. And I'm in heaven, I'm eating all those little candies, and rolling them around my tongue. But this takes a very long time. I don't care.

I forget about what she tells me about hurrying. I'm having so much fun. The shopkeepers are talking to me, teasing with me. The food smells good in my arms, the candy tastes good in my mouth. No one is yelling at me for a few minutes. These minutes, I feel happy inside. I am not thinking about my sister, not at all. That's my problem. I can never keep these things in my head.

When I get back home finally, I see my sister in the doorway and she don't look happy.

Uh-oh, I think. This is not good. I've taken a very long time. Hours. Andu will be here soon, and she isn't ready yet, she's behind schedule. She's furious.

She pinch me and grabs the food out of my arms. One of the tomatoes falls, rolls on the ground and splits open. Red juice runs out like blood.

She looks at me, murder in her eyes, but she can't do nothing because she has to concentrate on getting ready. My sister's sons giggled evilly at me. They are hungry too and no one is happy with me. So you can see, this is not a very good beginning to Andu' s visit.

When he gets there I'm excited to see him and I run and hug him. His wife, the one that used to lock me out of the house is there, holding their baby. It's a little girl and by now she's really a toddler, maybe two or three.

"Hello, Ghabriela," the wife say, sort of nasty, or at least that's the way I hear it.

"'Lo," I say back, not looking at her.

It doesn't matter what I think, because the place is filling up with people. We got relatives and neighbors and everyone is visiting and eating and drinking. Although I'm happy Andu is here, I'm not in a very good mood. I just been yelled at and pinched over the food thing, and I'm not happy to see Andu's wife prancing around.

Everyone fusses over the baby, and the wife shows her off. She shows the little clothes she has sewn for her and the little ornaments she has put in her hair. I'm feeling madder and madder at everyone, especially Andu's wife. If she'd been nicer to me I wouldn't have wound up here. I hate her.

I'm just sitting on the stairs watching everything, when a woman who is brushing the little girl's hair brings her over to me. I think she is just trying to be nice to me, trying to include me. She shows me how to brush the hair, too.

At first I'm sitting there, brushing her hair, being nice, making those noises everyone makes to babies. And suddenly, for some reason, something in me takes over. I don't know why. Anger washes over me. No one brush my hair, no one fuss over me. Maybe all that anger at everyone just come up, maybe I want to get back at Andu's wife, the girl's mother. To this day I don't understand it, but instead of brushing her hair, I push her. All of a sudden she fall down the stairs. Everyone stop talking. They run to the baby to see if she's okay. She's bruised a little, but otherwise she's fine.

Then they all are looking at me, screaming, talking fast.

"Why did she do that?" they ask. "What is wrong with her?"

My sister starts yelling at me, telling everyone around her how evil I am.

They all agree, the devil is in me. And my sister threaten how she'll beat me later, and the other women all start asking things like, "Ghabriela, why did you do such a terrible thing?" and the yelling and the noise start to make my head hurt. Everyone is just yelling and yelling, except my brother.

He come over to me and he talks quietly to me. He explains that just because someone treats me bad, don't mean I have to take it out on this little girl. He understands. He is the only one who doesn't yell. His voice is quiet, deep. He is calm and he loves me even though I have done something bad. His disappointment is worse than all the beatings in the world can ever be. Then he gently takes my hand and leads me away to a quiet corner in the kitchen to get me away from everyone. We both sit on the floor.

He says softly, not raising his voice, quietly so my head stops hurting and I could listen, "Ghabriela, this isn't the kind of thing you want to do."

I just look at him.

"You know if you do things like that that is what people will remember about you. You don't want this little girl thinking of you as someone who hurt her, remembering you that way, do you?" he asks me gently.

I shake my head.

"Of course you don't," he says, kindly, giving me a hug. "You want her to remember you being kind, and generous to her."

I nod.

Then he sits back and sighs. "I know things haven't been easy for you since Mamma died. And I know my wife don't treat you very well. But you don't want to hurt a little girl for what her Mamma did. She never did nothing bad to you, did she?"

"No," I say in a whisper.

"Well then, you want to be remembered as doing the kind thing. I know you are that way in your heart Ghabriela. So you need to act that way."

Tears rush into my eyes. I hug him. I want to go hug the little girl, but no one would let me near her. But in that minute, I decide that I wasn't going to be the kind of person that hurt people. That day my brother made me think about something I have never thought about, about the person I want to be. His words stay in my head forever. Really, that conversation changed my life. As I grow up I think about what he said, about how I want people to remember me. And when I think back on it, what makes him even more wonderful, was he knew to say all this when he was only still in his teens.

We go back to the party and I spend the rest of the time in shame, my cheeks burning, and the grown women are all looking at me and clucking their tongues. I see people staring at me. My sister just shakes her head at me. I see her talk to someone else. I hear her say, "She's evil, that one. God knows what she will do next."

"She's dangerous," the other one agrees.

My sister nods her head. "I'm afraid to have her around the other children." Everyone is sympathetic to her, and the burden she has to bear.

My brother leaves the next day, and no one says nothing about the party. But I think it was that incident that started me on the road to the orphanage. That and Mamma's dream visits.

CHAPTER

5

One day, not so long after Andu' s visit, I wake up and my sister says to me, "Here, put your stuff in this bag." She hands me a sack, like for potatoes or something.

"What stuff? Where are we going?"

"Never mind where we are going. Just put all your stuff in here," she say.

Well, I don't have too much stuff so this isn't going to be hard. I got some clothes. I got the pair of shoes to wear. That's it. I put the clothes in the bag.

She grabs me by the hand.

I don't get to say goodbye to anyone. I don't get to do nothing.

She brings me to this building. It's like maybe a school would look. There are a lot of kids living there. I don't like it. It kind of smells funny, so many kids and all. It don't smell like home.

My sister tells me to go sit in a chair, while she talks to the woman there. There is a woman, maybe middle age, I don't know. She and my sister sit in her office and talk.

I can hear some of the things my sister says. She tells her I belong to some woman that works for her, that the woman's husband, my father, just died in an accident. The woman can't take care of me, she tells the orphanage lady. She don't have no money, no family. These are all lies, stories she tells so she can leave me at the orphanage.

The woman and my sister come out of the office. I try to hide behind my sister. I'm a little shy. I don't want her to leave me here.

I start to beg her, "Don't leave me, I'll be good." But she just pinch me to be quiet and I am.

The woman comes over to me and says my name softly, "Ghabriela, hello."

"'Lo," I say back.

She smiles kindly. "I know this must be a hard time for you. I'm sorry to hear about your daddy."

I don't know what she's talking about so I keep quiet. I kind of twist my foot a little, and I twirl my hair with my finger.

"You know we have lots of children living here. I know there are some other little girls your age. I'll take you around to meet them."

I nod.

"I'll show you around first, and show you how we do things around here, tell you the rules."

I'm thinking I'm not going to like this one bit. But the lady is okay, nice enough. She don't yank me or pinch me. She treats me with kindness. She shows me the main room where the children spend time.

"We do lots of things here, like macramé, and sewing and drawing," she says. "And don't worry, we'll teach you how to do all this. You look like a fast learner to me," and she smiles and I smile back. She shows me some of the stuff the kids do. It look pretty good to me. I don't know if I'll be able to do it.

Then she takes me out to the yard to show me the children and where they play. It is recess now and everyone is out there. The kids are playing games I know, like hopscotch. They throw around a ball, that kind of thing. Nothing fancy, but it's okay. She introduces me to some other kids my age. They ask me to play with them and I do.

When I turn around my sister is gone. She don't say goodbye, nothing. I'm there forever. This is where I live.

Later on, one of the women shows me my bed and my little cubby to put my things in. Everyone have exactly the same thing – same type of little bed and same little cubby, so I don't feel different from everyone. That night, though, it's hard to sleep. There are maybe twenty other little girls in my room, and our beds are all lined up. I lie in bed and hear everyone breathing. My bed is at the end of the line, near the wall. I can't sleep and I run my hand along the wall and it feel cool. Somewhere in the middle of the night I hear a kid cry and some adult comes over and takes them out of the room, talking quietly, but in a stern voice.

Once I get used to it, in some way I like it better than being with my sister's kids, because we are all equal. No one cares about any of us, but at least we are in the same boat. Those first few weeks are rough, especially at night. I am in a totally strange place. Nothing familiar is there. I don't really know anyone. I can't go outside and wander around the streets like I do at home. I can't steal fruit from the neighbor's fruit tree or go to the store to get a sweet. I'm just there, away from everything.

There are some grown-ups there to take care of the kids and they are not bad to us. They just don't care. They like to have time to gossip, to drink coffee, to nap in the hot afternoons. As long as we don't bother them, they don't bother us. The problem though, is they never talk to us. I want to talk to some grown up, I want someone to notice me, to take care of me.

Whenever I get a chance to talk to one of the teachers, I sit as close as I can, and smile big as I can. I notice their earrings, I play with them, tell them how pretty the earrings are. Still, I never get the feeling they feel that way back, that they want me that close. But I don't care. Nothing stop me. I take things into my own hands. I'm plenty inventive, even back then and think of all kinds of ways to get their attention. One way I think of is by getting sick. No one can ignore a really sick child.

The advantage of getting sick is not only that the grown-ups will have to pay attention, but that the nurse, who's really, really nice will have to take care of me. I know the nurse a little, I see her now and then and she seem nice, young, and pretty with a good smile. I admire her; I want to get to know her. I want her to like me.

One day, I think if I run a fever, they will take me to the infirmary. I lie in the sun one afternoon, hoping to get very hot. Then I call my friend, Viola. I tell her I'm burning up with fever, I feel so hot, so sick. She should run and get someone quick, I say.

And she does. She gets one of the ladies. The lady runs over and she feels my head, looks at my throat, talks to me. She shakes her head. "Nothing wrong with this one," she say. I hear her laughing with her friend. "Got to keep an eye on this one," she say.

One thing about me, I'm determined. I can see the lying in the sun thing don't work. I give it up for a while, but then I start to feel desperate for someone to pay some attention. I know I can figure something out. I sit the field, try to think about what I can do, how I can take things into my own hands. I see a cactus growing there. I think, if I put the cactus needle in my eye for sure they'll put me in the infirmary.

I'm young, not thinking I could be blind. Not thinking ahead. I think that gets me into trouble a lot of times in my life.

So, without thinking, I push the needle into my eye. That gets everyone's attention for sure.

They rush me over to the infirmary. The nurse stays calm, but everyone else is yelling. How could this happen? It turn out, though, I'm lucky. It's not serious. The needle stays on the edge and just kind of irritated my eye. No damage.

My methods are not too sophisticated, but I am never content to just let things be, let life unfold. I always got to make things happen, figure out what I want, and go for it. Maybe it was because I knew no one else was going to do it for me.

So after the thing with the cactus, no one take me serious if I complain about anything. But things change a little. I notice the nurse goes out of her way to say "hello," be friendly. I think she understands a little.

Things go along, and I get pretty used to living there. I got some kids to play with, I got my bed. I don't have a lot of things, but I have what everyone else has, and it's enough.

What I don't have is someone to care about me, to wonder how I'm doing, if I'm dead or alive. It kind of gnaws on me, that I got no one. But I find out about then, that the one thing I got is stories. I got a good imagination and I can make up stories for everyone. I get pretty good at it, too. I always know what they want to hear. If there's one kind of story kids at an orphanage want to hear, its stories about families.

Now, where am I going to get these wonderful stories about families? Well, for one thing, I always keep my eyes open and watch what other people do. When we go into Asmara, I watch the rich European families, the dressed up mammas and their little kids, and even the nannies. I watch how people dress, I watch how they do their hair, how they walk. Sometimes I even follow a little and listen to what they do, how they spend their time. I hear stories about going horseback riding. I hear stories about lying around on their yachts.

So I make these stories up. I get a little circle of kids around me, and I start describing in detail my rich wonderful family. I tell about the perfume they wear, the jewelry they have. I tell about the horses they ride, and the boats we go on and how fast they are. The kids sit and listen, mouths open, you couldn't get them away from me for nothing in this world. And they never ruin my story, never say, "How come you here then, if you got such a wonderful family?"

And I got something else that help me with my stories. We see movies. There in the 1950s in the middle of Eritrea, they take us to see movies almost every Sunday, usually Doris Day movies, if you can believe it. Well, it's not always Doris Day. But the movies are almost always American or Italian. And believe me, we don't understand a word of them, but we love them. We look forward to them. We trade stories about what we think the movie is about. We make up long complicated plots to match the pictures of Rock Hudson and Doris Day.

And we sing *Que Sera, Sera*, "whatever will be, will be." We also learn *Frere Jacques*, in Tigrinya, the language we speak in Eritrea. I don't know where that come from, but to this day, I can sing *Frere Jacques*.

Sometimes, we get lucky and the movie is really interesting. We don't sleep for a week after we see the movie about the one-eyed monster. We walk back from the movies, all of us in a line, walking the couple of miles home as it starts to get dark.

All of a sudden, I lean over and I whisper in my friend's ear, "Watch out, there's something with…" and then I scream loudly "ONE EYE run for your life," and everyone starts to scream and giggle and the grown-ups shush us up.

And every night, they read stories to us. They read us from a book called *Treasure Island*. The woman who reads to us is also a teacher and she can translate from English. So we hear the real story in Tigrinya.

I love those stories. I make up pictures in my head, and I imagine myself on wonderful adventures, being very brave and making things work, making a life out of nothing. I got to tell you, we all love those stories, and we can't wait to find out what will happen.

So it goes on like this. I learn to do things during the week, mostly handcrafts, sewing, that kind of stuff. We don't do much with reading or math. They try to teach us a little, but I guess they figure it isn't gonna do us much good. And besides, they can sell the handcrafts we make, so it helps out. During recess, we play games, and at night, they read us a story before we go to bed. We got a regular routine going during the week and on Sunday, we go to the movies.

It's Saturday, though, that's the heartbreaker. Saturdays are bad. I can't tell you how upset I get on Saturdays.

When the weekend comes, every Saturday usually people come to visit their nieces, or their cousins in the children's home. But here I am alone, nobody, nobody comes to see me. Sometimes I just stand by the window of the big room, my nose pressed up against the glass and I watch all the families. But no one comes for me. Sometimes I go to the infirmary and try to get the nice nurse to talk to me. If she isn't busy, she let me hang out there a while, help her out.

But this doesn't stop me from thinking about the visitors I will have. I make up stories for the other kids about this. I brag to them that when my sister comes, my brother comes, they will bring me food like spaghetti and meatballs. It will be the most wonderful food anyone ever tasted. I describe this food to the kids, how it look, how it taste, how it smell, until saliva is running down their chins just from thinking of it.

One day, I am telling them about this miraculous food when the nun comes over.

She tell me, "Ghabriela, you got a visitor."

I act like this is the most expected thing in the world, even though I'm in shock. I can't believe it. My sister, she don't live that far away from me, not far at all, but she don't visit me. But there in the courtyard, is my brother and sister with a big basket of food. It's like the heavens open up for me.

My brother and sister have come for a visit. My brother try to make the trip from Tagrid to Asmara to see the family about once every other year, and when he comes, he wants to visit me and makes my sister visit, too. So there he is, smiling his beautiful smile.

He opens his arms to hug me.

My sister is carrying a big basket of food. She doesn't say nothing, but I can smell that food. Now for all the heartbreak I had with my sister, one thing I got to tell you is that woman could cook. She make some Ethiopian stuff, but since her husband was Italian, and since there were a lot of Italians in Asmara, my sister make Italian food too, or combined the ideas of both types. They had a kind of Italian way of eating. Nowadays, the fancy restaurants would call it fusion, but we didn't have a special name for it. But I cannot tell you how good that food was.

In the orphanage, we never get any special food. We get bread, sometimes vegetables they cook into a stew, but nothing really good. So I am not used to this. So we have our picnic, and I eat the food, the meatballs. They are so good I can't believe it. Somehow I want my friends to know about this. I don't know why exactly. Maybe I think they won't believe my family really came to visit me and brought me such wonderful food. Or maybe I just want to share this experience. Want them to taste the food I taste, know what it is like to. Maybe it's a little bit the same reason I want to tell my story, to share something I feel.

I sit there with my sister and brother in the area just outside the children's home and I cram as many meatballs into my mouth as I possibly can and eat them as fast as I can. My brother smiles at me.

"Slow down," he says softly, "we will be here a while. You will get as many meatballs as you want."

My sister doesn't say much. She looks bored and hot, which of course in Eritrea is not such an unusual thing.

My brother tells me some stories from back home, and jokes with me, asks me how I'm being treated.

I tell him people are okay here, but I miss him, which is the truth.

My sister pokes him and says, "I told you she is doing okay here. Mamma don't visit me no more in my dreams."

I look at them, because I don't understand what she means.

My brother laughs a little. "Seem like our Mamma been worried about you," he says. "She been coming to visit Gelila in her dreams every night saying how worried she is until you came here. Now, she doesn't visit much, and when she does, she seem calm."

My sister just nods.

I don't know what to say, so I just consider this a while. Mostly though, my attention is on those meatballs.

After a little while it's time for visitors to leave, and I know I have to go back to my friends, my usual life.

I have just been telling my friends about these wonderful meatballs my sister used to make and I desperately want to bring the meatballs back, but I know no one will let me, so I hide some meatballs in my cheeks. I save one on each side of my mouth, so I can give it to my friends to taste. I must have looked like a little chipmunk. They must have thought, *What a strange child is this Ghabriela.* But I keep these meatballs in my cheeks till my sister and brother leave.

Then I run back with them to my room to get my two best friends. I carefully take the meatballs out of my cheeks and wrap them up in a little piece of cloth. We all go to the play yard. I gather around me a little group of kids I know pretty well, maybe six or eight kids.

I whisper to them that I have something very special to give them. I tell them how I have these wonderful meatballs, they taste like nothing they have ever tasted in the world. I take them out from the cloth and hold them in my hand, like they are precious nuggets of gold. We all stare down at them. I divide the meatballs up, and we pass them around and we share.

Everyone is totally amazed at how good they are. I am a hero.

I remember that moment. I remember how good it feel to give them a present, to give them food, to be the one having something good to offer. That feeling will stay with me, and later, I will be the one who loves to share things, to make things for my friends, to give parties. It's that feeling that is born that day.

CHAPTER

6

One day when I was about nine years old, I sit in the play yard with my best friend, Viola. We just sit there with a stick making pictures in the dirt, not doing much of anything.

She points to some houses across the way, and starts to giggle, "You know who live in those houses?"

I sit back to think about it. I didn't know, but I don't want to let on.

"The *Invalides*," she whispers. I just look at her.

"They are missing arms, sometimes legs, too," she says.

"Why? What happen to them?" I ask. I had seen men like that close by here. They were sad looking, men with one arm and one leg only. Some of them had crutches, some crawled on the floor, using arms, legs whatever they got, some got carried around.

"We'll go over and ask one of them," Viola says.

I look shocked. "We can't just ask them," I say.

"Sure we can. We can sneak through one of the holes in the fence," she says.

Just then one of the grown-ups came by and sees us crouched by the fence watching.

"You girls get away from there, you got no business there," she growls.

I nod and Viola and I get up and sort of amble on a little like we're going to move on. Then, my curiosity gets the better of me. I say to the grown-up, "I seen the men that live over there, and I know some of them got only one leg, one arm. How come? What happened to them?"

She looks at me, like she's deciding what to say. Finally she tells me, "Those are the soldiers that got hurt in the war. Now go back to the play group," she says and she goes back to the building, watching us just long enough to see that we were heading in the right direction.

In all my years there, I never heard anyone talk about it. People just accept it. That's the way life is and you'd better get used to it. *Que Sera Sera*, whatever will be will be. At the time I had no idea about all the wars and all the troubles that Asmara went through over the years. I had no idea of Ethiopia's history, no idea at all.

When she was gone, Viola and I just look at each other, and turn back to watching the area beyond the fence, hoping to catch a glimpse of the men. We know no one will be looking for us for a while.

Finally, Viola says, "Lets sneak out, okay?"

I poke her and giggle and say, "Sure."

Viola and I are among the older children now, and we've been here almost the longest, so we know all sorts of things about getting around loopholes. We are resourceful, and we know where to go. So we do. We go over to the buildings where these men live.

There was a bunch of men, sitting outside, in front of the compound, playing cards. They are all missing arms or legs, sometimes both. Some held the cards in the one hand they had, or held them with their feet. It was a very strange sight.

From time to time, when we were bored, Viola and I would sneak over there and just watch the men from the edge of street.

Most of the men played cards, but there was one man who used to sit in his chair and whittle birds with a stick. He'd make all kinds of birds, all looking like they just about to fly. One day we crept closer and closer and he see us watching him. He smiles a little at us and ask us if we want to see the birds he is making. When we get closer, I see he is a kind and gentle person. He has a smile that reminds me of Andu. Somehow, when I think of soldiers, especially soldiers without arms or legs, I think they are going to be fierce people, but he seems so gentle. It surprises me, and I think about that, about the way people aren't always the way you think they gonna be.

I want to ask him questions about what happened to him; I always want to know things. He sees me staring at his arm where it's cut off, and his leg. He knows I want to ask. He says to me softly, "I don't talk about that. Ever."

I nod. Even at this age I understand. I understand there are just some things too terrible to talk about.

"How can you whittle with just one hand?" I ask.

He smiles. "Well, I whittled before this happened, so I just figured out a way. You'd be surprised, there's a lot of things you might not think you can do that you can, if you think about it."

I could see he had a board to hold down the wood and worked with his good hand.

"Here," he says, "Would you each like one of these?"

And he gave me and my friend each a little bird to keep.

We never see him again.

I stay at the orphanage a long time, long enough to see people come and go, changes here and there. First we do things one way, then a new group come in and we do things another way. Me, I just watch and I take it all in. When I first come there, the people running the place were just workers, it seem to me. They're okay, but they're not very interested in us. They got a job, they do it, more or less. I don't think they are mean people, and I don't think they are really kind people, just people with lives to live.

But after I was there for some time, things change. The nuns come to run the place. The nuns were nice enough, maybe even a little more caring than the people who'd been there before. I notice, though, that sometimes the nuns give treats to the kids they favored. Mostly they give them to the Catholic kids. I'd notice that hand go in the habit and put a little something in some grimy hand belonging to some little kid who'd break out in a grin. I'm telling you, I didn't get that candy very often. For a while I really, really wanted to be Catholic, so the nuns would have those hands swoop over and leave some candy. I prayed to God to be Catholic but nothing ever happened.

One afternoon, I say to Viola, let's go to the church next door. Viola look at me like I'm crazy, but she always up for an adventure. We sneak over to the church and lie in the grass right outside, in the back. We figure we close enough to the church, God can hear us. We lie there a long time and listen to the wind blowing and tell each other stories about the Virgin Mary coming to save us. Then we prayed to God to make us Catholic so the nuns would give us candies and like us special. Nothing happened though, at least as far as we could tell, so we give up after a while and just went back to the children's home, being our same old selves.

During the time I was at the children's home, official-looking people start to poke around. I hear the nuns whisper to each other, and they'd poke us and tell us to stand up straight. I could tell they want to make a good impression on these people. And these people didn't look like regular every-day people you'd see in Asmara at the shops. They look proud, and they wear different clothes and sometimes talk different languages and they looked different. Later on I find out that the United Nations start to take an interest in our orphanage, and they send people to look at it. It was about then that things improved, too. We began to go places, have more picnics, go on more field trips.

I don't change much, though, and I remember one day I try to smuggle chicken wings back from the picnic. I couldn't stand the idea of that last piece of chicken just getting put away, so I stuffed one piece of delicious, greasy fried chicken in my pocket. Oh my goodness, what a mess it was. I can't tell you how annoyed the nuns were, when they see a big grease spot spreading over my dress.

One of them say to me, "Girl, what is wrong with you, what are you thinking, putting fried chicken in your pocket?"

I didn't say much, just look at the floor, and wonder if she going to take my chicken away. She did. And for good measure, she say to me, "And don't be thinking we're going to run and wash that anytime soon. It will get washed when everyone else's does."

I didn't say nothing. There were lots of kids in the orphanage and no washing machines. In those days, everything was washed in a barrel with a washboard and soap. It was a big job, so staying clean was considered a big virtue. I had to wear that dress with the grease spot an awfully long time before it got washed. But when I think back on it, I guess that was fair. She didn't beat me or make an example of me or do anything terrible. I definitely didn't make any friends on that one, but she didn't do nothing bad to me.

It was sometime about then that there began to be talk about people from Saudi Arabia coming to adopt us. For weeks there are rumors. Rich people, with elegant dresses, and gold bracelets, they are going to come and take us away to somewhere wonderful. Remember, I always want to see the thing I don't know. And besides, everyone was talking about all the wonderful things that would come into our lives. I dreamt at night about it. I dreamt I went to a wonderful place with marble floors and all the food I could eat — great food, food I could smell in my dreams. I dreamt about fresh bread with fruit jam slathered all over it, and those little sugar candies, and fruit pies. Oh my, those dreams were so real I could smell the food when I woke up. And I dreamt about having beautiful clothes to wear and waving at my friends who still lived in the orphanage but came to visit me anyway. But most of all, I dreamt about having a mother. In my dreams she was kind with a soft lilting voice, and she always told me how beautiful I was.

Finally, the week arrived when the visitors come. There were preparations for days. People scrub the floors, and wash our clothes and the chefs ran around making wonderful food. When they arrived, it was just like I had dreamed. The women were wearing beautiful clothes and jewelry. But they didn't speak Tigrinya, they spoke Arabic. I never thought in all my dreams they would open their mouths and I wouldn't be able to understand them. But it was just a minor problem in my plans to go home with a beautiful lady and become a princess. I could overcome that.

They would have adopted me too, but there was some problem about letting us go to another country. We were Ethiopians the government said. We were born Ethiopians, and should die Ethiopians, if need be. I didn't know what was going on. I just knew I was going to stay at the orphanage, eat the same old food, watch the same old legless, armless men from the gate, do the same old crafts. That was it.

I can't tell you how depressing that was.

So it look like I'm gonna stay in the orphanage for a long time, at least until I'm thirteen. When you are thirteen, you are pretty much considered an adult and you got to take care of yourself. That seemed like a long time away most of the time I'm there. I don't think about that when I'm living in the orphanage. I'm just doing my thing, getting along, sewing, doing macramé, weaving stories for the kids and helping out.

If I think about my future at all, it's mostly about how I'm going to be a pretty lady, and marry a handsome man and have kids and beautiful house. That's it. I don't think about how all this is going to happen, no not at all. Mostly I just go about my business.

I still get the little children around me, but my stories have changed a little over time. I'm older, I got bigger ideas. I know more about the world. And the way I'm looking at things is changing. Instead of telling them stories about the terrific family I got who take me for vacations horseback riding and going in our yacht, now I make up stories about how our lives gonna be, the terrific families we will make for ourselves. I make up stories about who we are going to marry, how we gonna live. All of us are still going to those Doris Day movies, so I use that in my stories.

One time when we all just come back from seeing a movie, I tell them stories about how we're gonna be living in the city, wearing pretty dresses and having handsome boyfriends. Now, in Eritrea people really don't have boyfriends and date like in the movies, like Doris day and Rock Hudson. You got to have someone in your family introduce you to someone, or they choose someone for you from when you're little. But it don't matter to me. I'm practical. I combine things. I tell them how I got a sister who knows this handsome man, and as soon as I'm old enough I'm going to marry him and we gonna live in a pretty little house with a white picket fence. I got it all down. It don't matter to me that where we live they don't have little houses with white picket fences.

That's what I'm going to have, I tell my audience. The little girls are staring at me, hanging on every word. We flouncing our hair, and shaking our heads, like we see Doris Day do. Our hair don't flounce that much, but we try.

I'm just really getting going on my story when one of the nuns comes to get me and says Sister wants to see me.

Oh my, what have I done now? I wonder. I don't say nothing, just get up with her.

I see out of the corner of my eye, her hand go into that big robe of hers and she fish out a little candy for the girl sitting at the edge of the circle. She is a Catholic girl, so she is all the time getting candies. Some things never change. The other kids don't say nothing, just pretend it's not happening.

I go through in my head all the things I could have done that week. Telling scary stories to the little girls, leaving the grounds to go into town and wander around, not finishing my work project. I don't know — they too many things to think about. I got a knack for getting in trouble, but not bad trouble. I try and get along. Mostly the sisters like me, although they always say to me, "We don't know what we gonna do with you, Ghabriela. You are a handful!"

I get up to leave, and the little girls pull on my dress.

"Oh, don't go, Ghabriela," they say. It's nice having people want to hear what you got to say.

I bend over and whisper loudly to them, "Later, I'll tell you how my story ends later," and I leave.

So I go to see Sister. She's in her room, and she is sitting behind a big desk. I'm sure when I think back on it, that that desk couldn't be nowhere as big as I remember it. But in my memory it fill the room, maybe even the orphanage. You don't talk back to a person behind a desk like that. I'm even starting to feel a little nervous inside, but she smile at me, so I figure I couldn't have done anything too terrible.

"Ghabriela, you are growing up," she says. "You will be thirteen next month."

"Yes, ma'am," I say. I wonder why she is telling me this. It's not like they will be planning a party for me. I never had a birthday party in all the years I can remember. No one has birthday parties in the orphanage.

"You're grown up now," she tells me. "You are too old to live in the orphanage."

I don't say nothing. I am shocked. I guess I know that at thirteen you are an adult, but somehow it just never really hit me. You'd think with all the stories I told I'd be thinking about the time I'd leave the orphanage, but I'd never thought about it any real way, except for marrying someone handsome and rich and wonderful. I just stand there.

She tells me they found me a job in a factory.

"It's a good job, too, Ghabriela," she tells me. "It pays a salary. A lot of people want a job like that. You see them wandering the streets now, more and more of them looking for just that kind of job."

It's true. I see when I go into town, there are lots of people from the countryside coming in, looking poor and scraggly and hungry. It hasn't rained for a long time, so the crops are no good they say. But me, I don't know anything about factory jobs. I don't know what to think. One thing about me, I'm always a good worker. I can do just about anything with my hands, make anything, and I'm fast. Sometimes I got a mouth, people say, but I'm a good worker.

Sister just look at me standing there, mouth open, hang dog look. I must look as shocked as I feel, because she say, "It will be all right, Ghabriela. I'll have someone take you over there to see what it's like, so you'll know. We'll arrange it for tomorrow."

So the next day, I put on my cleanest dress, comb my hair, try to look my best. Sister Maria comes and takes me to the bus stop. We ride together to the factory.

I couldn't believe it. All around there was white in the air, like clouds, but it was hard to breathe. I can remember that feeling, of not getting enough air in, no matter how I suck through my lungs. They make white thread in the factory and they turn it into clothes, so there's all this stuff floating in the air. I watch. I think I can do this okay. Look hard, but what choice do I got? Doesn't matter what I tell the little girls, no Rock Hudson is coming for me.

But that's not the worst news. Really — it gets much worse. I'm going to go back to live with my sister. I need to live somewhere and the orphanage director called Gelila and told her to take me. I know the orphanage director have to convince her to take me back. I know because we didn't leave each other on any good terms.

"I don't know," my sister told her, "what will I do with her? Besides, Ghabriela is thirteen years old. She can be on her own. I don't need to take care of her anymore."

But somehow the nun convinced her to take me in. She explain I would be making a paycheck now, that I could turn it over to her and I wouldn't be a burden to her anymore. I imagine this sounds better and better to her. So I got sent back to live with her. The three kids are still living with her, the two boys about my age, Abel and Salameh and the girl, Genet, who is younger.

CHAPTER

7

I desperately don't want to go back to live with my sister, but what choice do I got? At least in the orphanage, we might not have much, but we are all equal. And I'm kind of a hero there. The kids love me, I'm the oldest, I tell good stories, I'm good at all the craft stuff we supposed to do there that they sell. I make the best sewing squares, and I braid hair and rugs really fast. They like me there.

I tell all my friends I'm leaving.

Viola puts her arms around me and gives me a hug. I got tears in my eyes; she got tears in her eyes. "I'm never going to see you again," she say.

I just hug her tighter, and don't say nothing. She probably right I think.

Once I leave her and go all the way to my sister's house, who knows what is going to happen? The little kids come up to me, too, and hide their heads in my skirt.

One little girl who I tell the best stories to and hug goodnight all the time, shyly holds out a hand to me, with her fist closed. I open it up, and there's a little candy in it. I know she has saved it just for me. I give her a hug. I will miss everyone.

Sister puts me on a bus and tells me the stop to get off. It is right near my sister's house and I will know the way.

All the time in the bus my stomach hurts. I don't want to see the house with its brick floors and nasty drain I got to clean all the time. I don't want to think about all the fights and the beatings. I just don't want to go there. I got no good memories. When I get off the bus, I find my way back to the house. I forget how beautiful it is in this part of Asmara. The houses look so pretty and all the little gardens invite you and it smells good with all the flowers. I forget about all that. The orphanage is okay, but it's not beautiful, doesn't smell like perfume and wonderful things cooking in people's houses.

When I get to the house, I take a deep breath and knock on the door. My sister open it, and she look the same. She don't look especially happy to see me, but she sighs and lets me in.

I see all her kids sitting there in the living room and I smell the food, and all of a sudden, it hit me, like in the stomach. They're all living together, cozy, a family, eating fresh baked *injera* and I'm sitting there all by myself in the orphanage, having nothing. That little ball of anger that always hide out in the bottom of my stomach starts to spread out. So I start off not being very happy.

But pretty soon, I got lots to be unhappy about. I'm not a special guest, I'm not loved; I'm Cinderella. They laugh at me. No one wants me here. My sister sees me as a burden to bear, a pain in the neck, a thorn in her side. And the kids take their clue from her. She lets them know without saying it, it's okay to bully me. She watches and never stops it, never says a word.

And Abel is really cruel. He thinks up terrible things to do to me, mean things. He's very smart and he uses this for his reign of terror. He pulls away my chair as I start to sit in it, he trips me, he pinches me under the table, he hides things I need to get ready for work. He tells lies to get me in trouble.

And he usually follows these deeds up with a terrible laugh. Years later, it will turn out that he is mentally ill. He will wind up spending most of his adult life in an institution. But then, for those years, no one understands how really sick he is. He is just another kid and I am his victim.

What I ask myself now, when I look back on it, *Why didn't the grown-ups stop him?* It is the question I think of over and over. It is the question that haunts me. People saw the cruel things he did, but no one did anything. I still get angry when I think of that. But maybe that's a question for everyone in the world. Terrible things happen all the time and no one does anything.

There is a saying I heard once that ten percent of people are cruel no matter what, ten percent are kind no matter what and the rest just follow along whoever they meet. I believe it. Too bad for me, Abel was in that ten percent cruel group, and I'm there with no one to protect me.

So now I'm living home. I have to take the bus to the factory and there are lots of girls my age plus some grown women. I get on the bus and I sort of like it because I get to know people. You know, same people there on the bus every day. The bus driver is nice and he jokes with me. But we don't go in the same time every day. I got three different shifts. Sometime, I go in early in the morning, sometime I go in late in the afternoon and sometime at night. Sometimes I'm so tired, I don't know what I'm doing. That's what I remember, always being tired.

I'm thirteen years old. I'm not going to school, not going to dances, not doing anything fun. I'm dreaming of a life with some fun, some music and some laughing. And worse, no one loves me, no one cares if I disappear off the face of the earth except for my paycheck.

The work is hard and I don't like breathing all that white powder, but after a while, I kind of get used to it. But my skin always has a white powder on it. It makes me lighter. I'm not sure what I think about that.

I look around and I see I'm the only one with no shoes. I don't have a pair. I work day and night and I walk from the bus to home and home to the bus, but still I got no shoes. To this day, I have a special fondness in my heart for new shoes.

But you know, I still have a good imagination. I used to make up stories at the orphanage, and I still think of stories to tell myself on the way home in the bus. When I get off the bus at night from the late shift, all my stories come out to scare me. Instead of the old Doris day movies, now I remember all the monster movies we used to see. I think "The Eye" is gonna get me.

Some of the girls, the lucky ones, have someone to meet them, older brothers, older sisters, when they get off the bus late at night. Me, I got no one, and I'm always terrified, walking in the dark, thinking of all the worst things that can happen. One night, I get home and it is pitch black outside, and the wind is moving the trees around, and the shadows are moving. The doors are locked but I usually just knock at the window and they open the door. But this night, for some reason, I feel scared to the bone. I don't want to go over to the window, because it's in the shadows, around the side of the house. I start to go there but I see something move. I think all kinds of terrible things. I can't help it, I scream, and I scream. I'm so scared I'm shaking and I can't stop it.

My sister comes out, the neighbors come out, everyone comes out to see who is getting killed, what all the noise is. But it's just me.

My sister starts yelling at me. "Are you crazy?" she yells. She so mad, she gives me a slap, and then I start to sob. She looks at me in disgust. "You're impossible," she tells me. The neighbors see it all and just shake their heads.

After this, nothing changes, I still have to work three different shifts, still have to come home all by myself in the dark. I think to myself there must be something better. In my heart I know people feel love for each other. Just not for me. Sometimes I wonder, what's wrong with me? No one loves me. And sometimes I'm just angry, just have rage in my heart.

Every morning I get on the bus. There are two women there I get to be friends with kind of. They like me, and maybe they feel a little sorry for me. They share some bread with me and fruit when I get on the bus in the morning. Sometimes when they have a little treat left over from supper and we're going home on the late shift, one of them gives me a bit.

And every paycheck, on the bus they have a lottery. Everyone put in some money, and one person wins it. Eventually, everyone wins at least once.

And when you win, you get a lot of money, enough to buy some really special things, some nice clothes and shoes. People on the bus don't think of it like gambling. They think of it like a savings plan. Keep playing the lottery, eventually you win, you get the things you'd have saved up for. But me, I don't have money for this. I watch other people chip in, get excited, win, lose.

One day Mekdes, the bigger woman, looks me up and down. She says to me, I see you working all the time. I see you on this shift, on that shift, on the other shift.

"Yes, ma'am, "I say, "I work pretty hard."

"How come you never have any new clothes, or shoes? And you never put money in the number pool. You always dressed like you never have anything just some old rags. And you so skinny."

I hang my head down. "I don't know," I mumble.

"Where is your money going? What do you do with your paycheck?" she asks.

"My sister takes it," I say.

"Well that's okay," she say, "but she's got to give you some of it. That's only fair. You need clothes. How come your clothes are always too big?"

I don't say nothing. My clothes are always too big because they are always handed down from my sister, my cousins, even sometimes neighbors. But I'm embarrassed to say this. I got pride. I think now these women meant to be kind in their own way, to tell me to stand up for what I need. But I just feel small, embarrassed. I start to feel uncomfortable on the bus, everyone commenting how I got no clothes, no shoes.

One day I ask my sister about the money. It's hard for me to do this because I know she is gonna be mad. But I kind of screw up my courage and ask, "Why don't I get some of the money I bring home?"

She tells me I hardly bring anything home anyway, it's hardly enough to cover my food. I don't think this is true, but she makes me feel bad. At work they don't pay by your time, but by the weight of what you make. You make more, you get more money, you make less, you get less money. She is nasty about it. I'm good for nothing she tells me.

So for a while I keep on with things, the job, the bus ride, the scary shadows. I still tell stories to the other girls at work and they like me. At home, there is no happiness for me. It's always "do this," "do that chore," "clean up this." I do housekeeping, I work. My life is nothing. My hands are cracking from being in cold water so much and I'm always upset inside. I go along like this for a while, but in my head, I know I can't live like this.

The final thing is when my sister's kids hook up electricity to my chair. The boys do it to be funny. They make a joke of me. I come home one night, so tired from work, my life so bad, nothing but work, no one care for me.

I sit in a chair, and oof, terrible pain. I jump, I feel all scared inside, and in pain, unimaginable pain.

The boys are laughing and laughing. It's so funny to see me jump. My sister don't even yell at them. It's okay to torture me.

That night I decide I need a plan to get out of there.

The next time we get paid, I don't go home. I keep the money in a little envelope and I stay on the bus past my stop. I get off the bus and I look around. There are a lot of buses going to all different places. I close my eyes for a minute. I decide nothing is going to be worse than where I am now at home. I decide to take a bus going to the Red Sea. I always hear stories about how nice it is there.

I can remember when I worked in the factory making thread, a friend, told me about her vacations with her family to the Red Sea. *What do I got to lose?* I think. So I give the bus driver some money from my pay envelope and I take the bus to the Red Sea to the town of Massawa. I am on that bus for hours, seem like.

I get off the bus and look around. I don't know where I'm going to go. I don't know anyone. I just stand there. Remember, I'm the girl afraid of the shadows.

I watch people go by. The town by the Red Sea is a resort area. Lots of happy people around, lots of tourists, people who are rich by the look of them, and a few people that look like they been drinking and partying. I just stand there, watching, but I'm thinking I got to do something pretty soon.

But just then, a woman comes up to me. She asks if I'm lost.

I tell her I got no place to be lost from, that I ran away from home.

"Oh, dear," she says, "Well, come along. I will bring you back to my place. I run a little restaurant, a bar. I can always use some help," she says, "And I got extra room, you can stay for nothing."

"Okay," I say. What choice do I have? And she seems nice. I'm happy to have somewhere to go. I don't think to ask her why she's hanging around the bus stop waiting for homeless young girls. I just go with her. Turns out, once more I go from the lion to the leopard.

This lady takes me to her house, where she makes extra money serving food and drinks. This place is on the Red Sea, near Massawa, so there are a lot of people that come by. There are tourists, and all kinds of people, rich and poor, and there are navy guys mostly from Eritrea. It's a busy place, everyone looking for something.

The place is simple, made of stucco, painted pretty colors, but she's right on the beach. You can hear the water slapping the sand from the bar. The sky gets streaked with colors as the sun goes down — reds and gold across the blue.

The guys that come in, though, they don't notice that much. They are looking for drinks and women, young girls. That's where I come in. I'm supposed to help the woman run the bar, serve the food, clean up. She is a busy woman, trying to scrape together a living. Her husband died a few years back, leaving her on her own. So her life is not so easy and she does what she can to make ends meet. And she needs some help, cheap help. If she hires young girls, we help just for someplace to sleep and some food to eat.

The men that come in like to hang around more if there are pretty young girls there. And the more they hang around, the more they buy to eat and drink. But sometimes, especially after they been drinking, they like to touch what they see.

So after I'm there for a few days, it gets to be the weekend and it's noisier and louder and people been drinking more. I bring one of the guys a beer and he cups his hand around my neck, strokes my hair.

I look down at the floor and back away. The guy next to him pokes him, say something like "She's just a kid, leave her alone. I bet she doesn't even bleed yet."

I don't know what they talking about at the time. Now I look back, I understand, and he was right. I never even had my period yet. I was that young. I don't know nothing about it.

But I come back with more food and more drink, and the same guy that been touching my hair puts his arm around my waist and pulls me in. I can smell the alcohol on his breath, and I feel uncomfortable. He tell me I'm beautiful and start playing a game, like "eeny, meeny, miney, moe" kind of thing with my breasts, tapping the nipple on each one. I get scared and I run over to the woman who runs the place. I tell her what he's doing, that he's playing with me, that I don't like it.

She looks at me in annoyance. "Honey, what do you think they come in here for? They want a little food, a little drink, some pretty girls around. So it kills you to let him touch your breasts? What's so special about your breasts any-way? Big deal. Grow up and don't come whining to me."

That's what she tell me. Well, I'm stuck here. I don't have no place else to go.

I ask one of the other girls about it. She's a lot older than me, maybe seventeen or eighteen. She laughs and gives me a hug. "Hey, honey, that's the way it is. Men like that. Just smile. But hey, don't let them do anything more, if you know what I mean, without getting extra money for it."

Well, I guess I'm not going to get any help for it, and I'm feeling more and more scared.

I don't know whether I would have gotten used to it or not, but one night, just about a week later, that same guy came in. He really liked me and he was determined to have me.

It was kind of a nice night out, you know moon and stars, real clear. There were some tables outside, and he sat outside, near the beach and he asked the head lady if I could serve him, so I had to bring him his beer and his food.

He puts his arm around me and said it was so beautiful out, we should walk along the beach. I told him I couldn't, I had work to do, and I start to look very busy cleaning up, but the lady says, "Oh no, Ghabriela can walk with you. Go, Ghabriela, take a walk with our very good friend. And when he come back, I'll have big meal and drink for him."

I feel chilled, afraid, but I go. I don't know what else to do.

We walk along the beach and he is kind of leaning on me, slurring his words, putting his hands all over me. All of a sudden his hands are on my breasts and I push them away.

He smiles, "What do you want to do that for? Don't you like me?" he asks.

I lie and say I like him fine. I just don't want him to do that.

He says, "It will feel good, it's a perfect night," and he slides his hand under my shirt and soon he is holding my nipple between his thumb and finger.

I wonder if this is what that girl meant about doing more. I don't know nothing, still.

"Oh, baby," he says, and he starts to breathe heavily.

We're not walking anymore, we're standing together and he all over me. I'm getting worried now, and he push me down on the sand and pulls my skirt up.

I start to yell.

"No, no, no don't yell, you will spoil it," he says.

I keep yelling, but I guess I don't spoil it enough, because he forces himself into me and I'm shocked. I can't tell you how shocked I am, and in pain. It hurts. I wonder if it's going to kill me. But when he's through he just fall asleep, right there in the sand.

I run back and tell the girl what happened to me.

She says, "That bastard raped you? Didn't pay you nothing? You should have gotten money from him." She's not upset about what he did only that he didn't pay me.

I'm upset. I'm bleeding, my clothes are torn. I tell the head woman what happened.

She shrug. "Hey, it's what men like to do," she tells me. As long as they buy the drink, buy the food, and pay up, it's okay with her. He is a good customer.

He comes in later and orders a big meal. She's happy.

I sit on a bench and sob. In that minute, I know nobody care for me, no one care what happens.

I run away. Again.

CHAPTER

8

So here I am, in Asmara and I'm totally alone in the world. I run away from my sister, I run away from the bar, I got no one in the whole world.

At first, I got no idea of what to do. I have a little bit of money from the bar and I find a place to sleep. It's common for lots of young women to get a cheap place, fifteen people to a room take turns sleeping there. So that's what I do. But as usual I keep my eyes open and I listen and watch.

I hang around downtown and I see that lots of women have young girls helping them take care of their children. If there's anything I know I can do, it's that. I always look after Genet when I lived with my sister, and in the orphanage I watch out for the younger kids.

Now, I just got to look responsible and find someone to hire me. I start asking around and it turns out, one of the girls I'm sharing a room with has a cousin who has a cousin who's looking for some help with her kids. You don't have to be rich to have household help. Just regular families often hire some-one to live in and help out.

The day I go to meet the couple, I dress up as nice as I can, I pull my hair back. I look pretty good. I go up to the house and it looks okay to me. It is medium size, painted a cheerful light green, and there is a small garden near the door. It's near town, and the man owns a shop in town, my friend told me.

I knock on the door and a comfortable- looking, pretty woman answers it. She got on nice hoop earrings, and a colorful flowing skirt, just like the one I'm wearing. She got two kids hanging on her, too, and they look sweet, like nice kids and there's two others playing in the room.

I can see the woman is pregnant, but it looks good on her. She looks healthy, up to the task of caring for all those kids.

This woman is older than me, maybe in her twenties and she already got four kids. She invite me in and offer me a seat. The floor is brick like in my sister's house. Everything looks neat and clean and smells good. It sure beats living in one room with fourteen other girls.

The woman has a nice smile, and she tells me she needs someone to help her with the children, and to help clean the house.

I say I will do that. I tell her I can help clean, and I can help cook the food, for sure. I know how to do a lot of housework type stuff from the orphanage and I'm good at it. I can tell she likes my enthusiasm.

She shows me the room I will get if I live there, and I'm thrilled. I can see I will have my own bedroom. It's small, but it has a little closet to hang my things and a little window. I never got my own room before. I share in my sister's house, I live with hundreds of kids in the orphanage, and then get a place on the floor at the bar. This is like heaven to me.

She introduces me to her husband and he seems nice, kind. He is polite to me, and treats me like a lady. He introduces me to each of the children.

They are young, the oldest maybe seven, the youngest about two. The two older ones, both boys, shake hands and smile, look shyly at the floor and giggle with each other.

I talk to them, make a little joke. I give them each a little candy I brought special for this. I remember from my orphanage days how far a piece of candy will go toward making a child feel good. A picture of the nun putting her hand in her robe and fishing out a piece of candy comes in my head, for just a second.

I see the husband and wife smile knowingly at each other, like they know I am the right one to take care of the children and help out.

The husband asks me to sit down and his wife brings me some coffee and a sweet.

The coffee is wonderful, and I have been smelling it since I walked in. The husband tells me they will be happy if I work for them. I will get the little bedroom the wife has showed me, and I will eat with them, and get a little pocket money besides.

So I'm lucky that I find this nice family and I agree right away to work for them. I don't realize how lucky it is to find that kind of work if you are a teenage orphan girl. Orphaned girls are the bottom of everything in life in Eritrea. Most girls with no families starve, get forced into the sex trades. Me, I do what it takes to survive, too, but I'm really happy that I find a nice couple looking for someone to help.

I start working for the family. The woman is patient and cheerful. She teaches me how to cook. She is a wonderful cook, and I love to help her cook. I don't mind doing housework now, because I feel like I'm helping her, not like she is forcing me. It's funny, but all my life I seen cruelness, and meanness, but I like to help. I like the feeling I get. Somehow I know kindness is going to be the only thing that make life better. I think I get that from my brother, Andu. Even now I can hear his soft voice when he tells me to think about how I treat others, how I want them to remember me. So I get that kindness from him. And maybe from God, too.

We go along like that and I enjoy the wife and the husband too. He is a nice person, helpful. Everything is going along good for several months. The wife is really showing now, she's maybe in her sixth or seventh month. She's moving kind of slow and pretty soon she won't be able to travel over bumpy roads.

It's usual for the woman to go back to her family, to have them take care of her when she's going to have a baby. So about then, the wife goes to stay with her family. The plan is that she is going to stay with them until after the baby comes. They'll help her when the time comes to have the baby and they'll take care of her for a while after.

Most people don't have babies in hospitals. There are hardly any doctors even if you want to see one. The hospitals are all overcrowded. No one is gonna go to a hospital if they're not sick, if they are just doing something natural like having a baby. Usually a neighbor helps, someone who has helped before. I guess it's kind of like having a midwife, but they don't really call them anything special. People don't talk about being pregnant there much. It's considered bad luck.

So the wife goes away to have her baby and she takes all the kids back to visit her family with her. So now it's quiet in the house and I'm home alone with her husband.

We joke, we eat dinner together. The husband, Ababu, has a small store, and I prepare breakfast for him and keep him company while he eats. I go to the shop to get fresh food for us and prepare it all. He treats me like an equal. One night Ababu comes into my room and sits on the end of my bed. We talk for a long time.

Next night he also comes into my room, and pretty soon, he is in my bed. But it isn't like the other time, the time on the beach. This man isn't drunk. He is respectful. He tells me he loves his wife, but she is not interested in him in that way since she been pregnant; she has other things on her mind. And now, she isn't even here.

I like him and it's cozy. It's been so long since I haven't been alone, since someone is nice to me, acts like they care. Besides this is the best place I have ever lived in. I'm comfortable, people treat me right, I got plenty to eat, anything I want. I'm thinking if I don't do what he wants, maybe he won't want to keep me around. I just want to stay there. So that's how it starts. And it keep on going. His wife is away a pretty long time. I hear she had the baby. Ababu goes to visit her and he comes back and tells me how cute the baby is, how healthy. He loves children he says, and he's absolutely thrilled.

It's hard to travel back and forth, so she stays there a while to be a little longer with her family. Her family, they see it as a blessing to have her with them as long as they can, to get to know the children.

But after some time, the wife comes home. She's busy now with the children, taking care of this and that and with the new baby.

I don't say nothing about her husband, and she don't say nothing. I don't think she knows, but maybe she suspects. It isn't unusual for that to happen there. Seems like people are okay with men having interests in other women, looking around, doing something here and there, as long as they stay with the family. That's the big thing. If they stay with the family, take care of everything, no one say too much. Oh, the neighbors might shake their heads, blame the girl a little. The wife will get mad, yell a lot, but in the end, people forgive these things. Everyone just tries to get through life.

Pretty soon I'm starting to put on some weight but I don't think too much about it. I loosen up my clothes a little. I put on more weight, and I think I have to eat less. I only got my period once in my life so far, so I don't think much about the fact that my period's not coming.

Pretty soon the neighbor women are poking each other and laughing when I walk by. Believe it or not, I still don't know what's going on. That's how naive I am. I notice that the wife is starting to look at me, a little hostile like, but she still don't say nothing.

Finally the husband says to me, "Ghabriela, you know, you are going to have a baby."

"I am?" I ask. I am very surprised.

"Don't worry," he says, "I will take care of you. But, I don't think it is good for you to stay with us anymore."

I don't know what to say. I haven't thought about this. He still is kind. He isn't mean or angry. He says he will find an apartment for me, and he does.

He gets me an apartment, and he gives me money to buy food.

I'm not unhappy that I can remember. I don't feel jealous. Maybe I don't expect anything of life no more. I don't know.

In the orphanage I used to dream about my little house with my children and my husband who look like Rock Hudson. But now I just try to survive. I don't think about the future no more.

He sets up the neighbor next door to look after me. She has a soft voice, and she's cheerful, and kind. She looks like what I dream a mother will be like when I am small. No, maybe not that she looks like the mother in my dreams, but she sounds like her, soft talking, cooing, encouraging me, showing things. Ah, where was she years ago when I was all alone in the orphanage? But of course, she isn't my parent, I'm not her responsibility. She treats me kindly because she treats everyone kindly.

She show me what to do to take care of things. She takes care of me. Sometimes, she and I and other neighborhood women gather in her kitchen to have coffee and gossip, swap stories. When it comes time to have the baby, the women tell me it will hurt, and I'm scared. I have enough things in my life that hurt; I don't need any more pain. They look at me knowingly.

This neighbor who takes care of me, she has a husband, and a son of about eight. One day, near to the time I am supposed to be having the baby, I go over to the woman's house and she prepares food for me. She shows me how to prepare food for when the baby comes. It is a tradition to make special foods for the guests who will come to see the baby. I'm not sure who will come to see my baby. I have no family, the baby's father will want to see it, but still that has to be done quietly. I make the foods anyway.

I am sitting there having lunch with this nice neighbor and her son and husband when my water breaks. I have no idea what is going on. But we shoo the little boy out of the room and the neighbor calls for the midwife, they put a fire on, they get something to tie the cord. By four o'clock the baby is there.

It turns out giving birth is nothing. After all the pain I'm used to, it's easy. And I have a beautiful baby, a boy. This boy is something. I am so excited, it's a feeling I don't understand. There is at last something of my own in the world.

The neighbor and I put out the spread for visitors. We make all kinds of special spicy food. And I do get visitors. The neighbors come, the baby's father comes. But my sister, she never comes at all. Of course, we haven't talked in a very long time, since I run away. But she knows where I am anyway, because there is a very good grapevine here. Seem like everyone know everyone's business. But still, we aren't in touch. I haven't seen her or her children since I left. It feel like they are from another time and place.

A lot of nights I sit there and sing softly to my baby. I stroke his hair. make faces at him and he make faces back.

The woman next door, Emebate, she shows me how to breast feed him, and how to change him and how to do everything for him. Women breast feed their babies anytime, anywhere.

I take him on the bus with me, I take him to the park. And I take care of him. I have money to take care of him, and time to be with him and my own apartment. I'm barely seventeen and I still have never had my period except once!

My life is going fast. I don't have time to think about what I want or don't want. But I am connected to someone and I feel happy inside, I know this is what I want — a family, a child, someone to take care of.

I go to the store to see the baby's father. The store he owns is nearby and my heart always feel glad when I see him. He has that gentle way about him and he's always happy to see me. His face breaks out in a smile, his eyes crinkle up with joy when I walk in with the baby. He always give me a hug, and always tickles the baby and gives him a kiss on the forehead. I feel like he's taking responsibility for the baby and me, and my job is to take care of the baby.

When I look back at it now, I know there are so many ways to see this time. In this country, now, he would be a criminal. He would be in jail for child abuse. I wasn't even seventeen yet when I first had sex with him. But then, in Eritrea, things were different. Girls with no families were like nothing in Eritrea then. No hope, no future, nothing. Family name was everything; that and money. But with no parents, no one stepping up for you, you just lucky to live.

And no one thought too much about it if a man had sex with a young girl. It's true religion was important, and of course it was against the religion to have sex with someone else when you were married, but as long as you stayed with your family, took care of them, no one said too much, just sort of pretended they didn't know what go on. It was bad luck to talk too much about it, anyway.

Wives looked the other way often. No one wanted to get divorced. I remember a neighbor of ours coming over to get some water. She had a black eye and we'd all heard terrible fighting the night before.

"Oh, it's nothing," she said. "I walked into something."

My nice neighbor just looked at me and shook her head as if to say, *Don't ask anything, don't embarrass her.* So I knew that there are lots of things you just don't talk about, and I knew you try to make your man look good.

So I never thought this man was doing anything bad to me. I didn't see him as taking advantage of me. He probably didn't either. It never even entered my mind. Me, I was happy that the baby's father was supporting me, and he wanted to see the baby. He was happy about the baby, played with him, cuddled him. I was glad I got to keep the baby too.

Sometimes, often, when a man fathered a child outside marriage, especially with a young single girl, the father would take the baby and have the wife raise it with his other kids. The wife accepted that, because what could she do? She doesn't want to lose her husband. And, often the girl was happy to give the baby up. You can't work when you have a baby. There was no such thing as child support, or if there was, I sure never heard about it.

So I felt as though the baby's father was really treating me good. In that time and that place, he was not considered a bad guy. I got to keep my baby, got to stay in a nice apartment, and my life was okay. I didn't think ahead. I never did at that time. And of course, I didn't talk about bad things or worries. It would have been bad luck. And besides, who wants to hear that?

And maybe things would have gone on that way at least for a long while if I hadn't suddenly fallen down sick right in the middle of the street.

CHAPTER

9

Who knows why it happened? But I fell down and I can't feel anything. My leg can't move. I'm paralyzed. I'm lying there on the street, breathing in the dust, my dress ripped in the fall. I feel panic inside. I try to move my leg, nothing happens. I can't feel nothing.

My heart is beating fast from being scared, for myself and for my baby. He is screaming too. No one knows what is wrong. People gather around me on the street. They try to help me up, they tell me to move my leg, but it's no use. Nothing happens.

I try to check my little boy to see if he's hurt, but I can't move enough to do it. I don't see any blood on him, but I can feel his heart beating fast too, and his screams echo in my ears.

I try to shield him as I fall. But I'm lying there in the dirt, the baby is crying, the neighbors are gathering. It's a sight. I feel scared, but I feel like I'm not really a part of my body. I'm numb and everything feels very strange.

I hear someone say, "Get her to the hospital."

I hear someone whisper that God is punishing me.

That thought goes around my head but I don't believe it. What have I ever done bad to God? In my mind I know I'm on God's good side. I pray to him every day, still like they taught us to do in the orphanage. I don't have any special priest come visit me, but still I keep God in my heart. *What does the person that say that nasty thing know?* I think. *She ignorant.* The thought floats around my head.

The word hospital gets through to my brain, though. I must be dying if they are bringing me to the hospital. In Eritrea, most time you go to the hospital, you don't come out.

Someone else says to find someone to take the baby. My neighbor runs out and I hear her pick up the baby and coo softly to him, she bouncing him a little.

I hear him stop crying, just kind of hiccupping a little. And me, I just lie there, can't do nothing else.

I hear people calling for the baby's father, and finally he comes. He talks softly to me, he sounds upset, and he clucks over me in distress. Finally he picks me up and takes me to the hospital.

I'm not sure what's going on. No one talks to me. I think I sleep through most of it. When I wake up, I am in the hospital, and no one I know is there. I cannot move, so I lie in the bed and look at the ceiling and walls.

The walls are white tile. There are two rows of beds, each have maybe twenty beds lined up against the wall. There are nurses moving briskly here and there, taking care of people. The hospital smells of disinfectant.

I worry about my baby, about how he is and where he is. There's no one around to ask.

Pretty soon the nurses strap my breasts down and put ice on them, because I am still making milk, and my breasts ache. But even after the milk stops, my heart aches. For the first time in my life, someone needs me, really needs me and wants me, and I can't be there. I can't move my left side, can't lift my arm or leg, can't sit up. My bed is closest to the door and every time it opens, a draft goes on me and I shiver, maybe because of the ice on my breasts. I don't have it together enough to tell anyone, I'm just lying there, shivering. I don't remember much of that time, but I remember hearing people moaning.

In the beginning, they feed me, they bathe me, I can't do nothing for myself. I feel panic, I don't know what is happening to the baby, don't know what is happening to me. I think about my baby boy and wonder how he's doing, who's taking care of him. I wonder what he's eating, since I had been breast feeding him, and no one is bringing him around to me.

Pretty soon the baby's father comes to visit me. He sits on the end of my bed and talks gently to me. "The doctors think you had a stroke," he tells me. "They don't know why, but there it is."

I ask about the baby. I want to see him, want to know he is okay.

"I can't bring him to you, Ghabriela. I'm not allowed. It's against the rules. Besides, you wouldn't want him in here, would you?" he asks, looking around.

And it's true, people are coughing, hacking up lungs sound like, people moaning. Don't want the baby to catch something, that's for sure. At that time lots of babies don't make it to their first year, anyhow, even if you're careful, so I understand. But that don't make it easier.

I ask him who will take care of the baby, and he tells me that he hired the neighbor to take care of my son. She will take good care of him, he tells me.

This makes me feel a little better, because I know she is a good woman.

During this time, all I think about is my son. I worry about him, I need him. But I am feeling really sick. In addition to the problem that I can't move, I start to have problems breathing, I'm gasping for breath all the time.

Turns out I got pneumonia. I got all that ice on my chest to stop the milk, and the damn door opening and shutting all the time right near my bed, giving me the chills. They decide to move me to the other side of the room where I won't get a draft all the time.

So now my bed is in the middle of the row and I got kind of a different view. I can see all the beds are filled with sick women. No one goes to the hospital there unless you are pretty close to dying. Some of them are old, some are young. I'm sure they all got a story, but honey, I'm too sick to hear any of them.

I start to feel better after a while, to be able to breathe, and soon as I can think, I think of my baby. It is so painful, but every time I ask to see him, people just hush me up. I am beside myself. The days go by slowly. At first, I am so sick, I don't notice that much. I can't even turn over. I can't take care of myself at all, can't do nothing. But, gradually, I get a little better. I can move my arm a little, I can move my leg a little.

They don't do anything special to help me get better, they don't do physical rehabilitation like they do now. But little by little, I start to be able to do things, move my leg, move my arm. I think maybe people are surprised. I don't think anyone thought I was going to recover. But like always, I got a strong will, and I want to go home and take care of my baby.

One day one of the nurses come in and sits on the corner of my bed. "Ghabriela, we can all see you are doing so much better. You can use your arm, move your leg, sit up, turn over. Almost everything getting better," she say.

I nod.

"You'll be able to go home pretty soon, to leave the hospital." I smile. I am still sick. I am still dragging my leg. But I can move now. I can walk, I can feed myself.

I think I will go back to my baby and to my nice apartment and nice neighbor. When they tell me I can leave, I just go. I don't have anyone to come get me. I still got just the old clothes I had, but they washed them for me.

I leave the hospital and drag myself back to where I used to live. My leg is still not working too good. I don't know what I'm thinking, I been gone for over six months now, and I guess I expect to see my apartment same as before. But I go to the door and someone else is living there now. I don't know her, she don't know me.

I lean against the door for a minute to think what to do, and I feel all of a sudden blackness roll in. I don't know why but I know something bad is coming.

I go to the neighbor's house, and she answers the door. I can see she don't want to look me in the eye. She always a good friend to me, but I can see, now she feels differently about me. I tell her my situation. I'm out of the hospital but I have no place to stay. I need to find someplace to stay and I need to get my baby.

"Can I stay with you just a little while?" I ask.

"You can't stay here," she tells me. "Why don't you go to your sister's?" she asks, not unkindly, but trying to keep a distance.

"How do you know I have a sister?" I ask. It turns out somehow she talk to my sister. Maybe my sister hinted about how bad I am, about all the terrible things I have done and not done, I don't know.

"Besides, I can't go to my sister's with a baby," I tell her.

Her face gets a funny look. She looks away.

I feel a shiver, and it makes me feel alarmed, something about how she looks. Something is not right.

"Where is my baby?" I ask, my voice loud.

Again, she don't look at me. "You need to talk to the baby's father," she says in a kind of low, muffled voice.

I can feel panic. I know something is very wrong. "Tell me, tell me!" I say to her, but she look at the floor, the ceiling, everywhere else but me.

"Talk to the baby's father. I don't know anything else to tell you," she say.

So I go down to the store to find Ababu. He look startled, like he see a ghost. Maybe that's how he feel. I don't think anyone ever thought I was going to get better, be walking around again. But after he covers up the shock on his face, he try to smile at me, seem cheerful to see me.

I ask about the baby, what I'm going to do.

He looks very upset. He takes my hand in his. He tells me the baby died. They did a tonsillectomy on the baby. It's very common to do in Eritrea, sometimes for no reason. And, he tells me, the baby got an infection and died.

"I didn't want to tell you when you were so sick," he says. "I didn't see the point to tell you just then. I'm so sorry."

I sit down on the step and cry and cry and cry.

In Eritrea babies die all the time. Lots and lots of them don't make it to their first year. But even though babies die all the time, I did not expect this. He was so beautiful, so healthy when I left him. But I believe Ababu. I never think for a minute there is any other reason I don't get the baby back.

But now, years later, when I tell that story to someone and they ask me, is there any chance the baby didn't die? Did they just tell you that? I am dumbstruck. All these years, I never think of that. I just believed what they told me.

I am completely grief stricken. I don't eat, I don't drink, I look at the walls in his store. Now I got nothing to look forward to. I just want to leave that place. I just want to get far away as soon as I can. And, I don't want to think about it, or talk about it. It will bring bad luck. But now that I think about it, how much worse could my luck get? I got nowhere to go now but back to my sister's. I'm not well enough to work or do anything right now, and I feel like I can't breathe here. I just drag myself away down the street, as fast as I can go.

CHAPTER

10

Even though they make me leave the hospital, I'm still not well. I'm still dragging my left side, I got no energy, I can't do the things I used to do. And now, stomping away from the store, knowing I got no baby, no apartment, no life anymore, I'm feeling sick, sick at heart, sick in my body. I think this the first time in my life when I feel really done in, beaten. Before this, I get angry, I sass back, I figure my way out of things. But suddenly, I got no energy for it, got no will. The hospital won't let me back and I got no place to go.

There is nothing to help you out if you are sick in that place at that time, no social security, no money, no nothing. You got to hope your family will help you out. And people beg or go into prostitution. That's it.

Somehow, I wind up on a bus, heading for Asmara, where my sister lives. I don't really think of it like a choice, a decision. It's like a force just pull me there. I got nowhere else. I can live on the street, or I can go back to my sister's house. Stuck again between the lion and leopard.

Let me tell you about my sister and me. We seem somehow locked together and neither of us can get away from the other. I remember someone once tell me, "God got a plan for all of us, and sometime got a lesson we supposed to learn. If we don't learn that lesson, we just got to keep having that same experience, over and over until we learn what we're supposed to out of it." I don't know what my sister or I are supposed to learn from each other, but whatever it is, we must have not been doing it, because no matter how hard we try, neither one of us can get away from the other. And believe me, we both try. But we're stuck together somehow.

When I get off the bus, I drag myself up to my sister's house. I'm not really thinking. I don't notice the little gardens, the flowers, the houses. I'm not seeing anything. I just want to lie down. I feel so sick, my side been feeling heavier and heavier. And anger is boiling up. What did she tell my neighbor? But somehow, even the anger is getting covered over, like covered up by some dark dust. I can't think, I can't feel, except an unbearable sadness.

My sister is not happy to see me, but she takes me in. She is not covered in this dark sadness that is closing in on me. She's angry and she can feel her anger. And she is not afraid of telling me about it neither. She's really angry, and things are now much worse between us than when I ran away the first time.

Remember, when I ran away from her before, I took the money from my paycheck with me, so she isn't happy with me. And at least when she took care of me before, I brought in money. Now I'm sick and I can't work.

My sister, she says, "Just look at you now. You run away. You make a mess out of your life, you're sick."

She's right. My life is a mess. I'm not yet twenty and already so much has happened. And I change in that time. I don't think of the future any more. I just think somehow I got to live. And some days, I don't even think that. Things between my sister and me go from bad to worse. But what can I do? I'm stuck. And I know, it's no use saying nothing to her.

She won't understand. Even then, I got a sense about those things, who it's worth telling your side of things to, and who you may as well save your breath, because they'll just argue with you. I have nowhere in the world to go, and I have no one who cares about me. And right now, I need love and care. I'm sick and I'm tired and I'm hungry.

At first, I just lie in bed, look at the wall. I don't care about nothing. But somehow, deep inside me, I know I got to get better to get out of there. I start thinking about what to do. I think mostly about my health, because if I don't get better, there's nothing I can do for myself. And the one thing I don't want is to be dependent on anyone, especially my sister.

I go to the hospital every day to see if they can do something to make me feel better. I want to stay there, but the hospital don't want to keep me anymore because I can move around, move my arm, my leg. They think there's not much more they can do for me.

I tell them they can't leave me this way, but it falls on deaf ears, no one cares. And now that I'm not in the hospital I have to go to the clinic part. First, I have to walk about three miles to get there. I'm draggin' my leg, it's hot, and I don't feel well. But I do it. Then I wait on line at the clinic. I wait for hours. I watch the people there. They don't look too good either. The people coughing, probably with tuberculosis, I don't know. There's people with open sores, and malnutrition, sick babies, everything. And, while we are waiting on line, no one talks about their problems. We try to put on a good face, not tell nobody your troubles.

Lots of days, I get to where it's my turn, I'm almost there, I see a guy come out in a white coat and that door close. They close for lunch every day at the clinic, and when that door closes, it's like a stake through my heart. They take a long lunch time in Eritrea. It's a hot country and everything closes in the middle of the day. Come back at three they tell me. I sleep in the street outside the clinic instead.

When I get to see the doctor, he don't pay much attention. "Take this," he says giving me some medicine. Usually they just give you shots of something and send you away. Whatever they give me, it don't help. I come back day after day. I can't go on, I tell them. I feel sick, my head hurts, I can't walk right. I tell this to them over and over.

In the clinic, you get a different person to see you every day, but I come back so often, I get to know the people. One thing about me, I want something, I keep at it. One day, the doctor there just look at me with an "Oh, it's you again," — look. I tell him I got to go back to the hospital I feel so bad. I know he thinks I'm a whiner, but finally he admits me. I will be someone else's problem if I'm an inpatient.

I stay in a couple of months. At least I'm not living with my sister. I start to get better during this time. I don't know why, but the hospital is less stress than living with my sister, and I get good food there. My strength starts to come back. My head is not hurting so much anymore, and my limp has gone away. I'm not dragging that leg anymore.

It's time to go out on my own, they tell me. I know it too, that I need to do something now. I know I can't go back to my sister's house. No way. It will kill both of us.

I sit on the hospital steps for a while, thinking what to do. I got no money, my sister is no help. I got no job skills. I can't face working in a factory right now. I don't have the strength. I don't know anyone to ask about a job working for someone.

One thing about me though, is I've always kept my eyes open, look around. I know there is a big U.S. army base in town. I don't know why there's a U.S. army base there, and I don't ask. I don't really think about it. I just know there's always lots of things going on there, lots of young women hanging around, lots of guys looking for things to do. There's a bunch of bars that have crept up around there, and plenty of movie theaters. It's loud and noisy and beautiful all at the same time, and I think, maybe that wouldn't be a bad place to go. Now that I'm feeling better, I want to have somewhere exciting to be.

I don't really have a plan in mind. Somewhere in the back of my head, I'm thinking maybe I can work in a bar or something like that. Besides, it's a place I never been and I'm always wanting to see something different. And with lots of young people there, I think maybe I'll find a place to fit in. Anything will be better than going back to my sister's house, and I can't just sit on the hospital steps forever.

The bar I go to is right outside the American base. There's a whole compound there, all grown up just outside the base — it's kind of its own little world. There are bars and movie theaters and all sorts of things American men like.

The first time I go there, I feel like I'm stepping off the planet to some other world. I like it, in a strange way. I feel free. No one is looking down on me because I don't have family, because I'm an orphan. No one is thinking in their head how I'm ruined and no one will ever marry me. No, here things are free and easy.

Music blares out from everywhere. You can smell hashish in the air. People are walking around in tie-dyed shirts with beads. And there are handsome young men everyplace you go. I feel like it's okay here. I don't have to ask my sister for money; I don't have to feel like Cinderella.

The G.I.'s got plenty of money to spend, and they are all homesick and lonesome and wanting a little company. It's easy to go to the bar hang around, pick up a GI, make a little money. There are lots of pretty young girls doing that and I can see that I can become one of them. The government looks the other way — less people they got to worry about feeding.

First thing I got to do I can see is to get someplace to live. I don't have no money but I hang around a little, watch what's going on. I always figure things out fast, just by watching. There are lots of young girls there my age, and I figure if I can make friends a little with some of the other girls, then maybe I can share something to start with.

Some of the women there I don't want to deal with at all, believe me. They look hard, sharp. But some are just regular people, and I can see they are like myself, been running between the lion and the leopard trying to find some peace in life, some way to survive.

One of the girls looks really familiar. I keep looking at her and looking at her. All of a sudden, I know where I know her from. She's from the orphanage, been with me there.

It's Viola, the girl I shared meatballs with, the girl that lay in the grass waiting for the Virgin Mary to come. I guess it's not so surprising she wound up here. I go over and tell her, "Viola, It's me Ghabriela!"

She light up to see me. "Ghabriela! How you doing girl?" she ask. Then she whisper, "And now I call myself Bobbi. It's kind of like um, a stage name. Do you like it?"

I laugh, "Sure. It sounds very, I don't know, like you a person that's been somewhere."

She laughs, too. It makes us feel like she has a secret, somehow. Like there is another side to her.

I tell her I'm doing okay, but I need a place to stay. She tells me I can stay in her place until I get set up. There's kind of a cubby in back I can sleep in. Not too good for business to have me around, but she says it will be okay for a little while, and then she'll help me find a place.

So that's how I get started. Once in a while I think about what I'm really doing and I feel bad about the idea of selling myself, but I don't have anything else. It's not like I have a lot of choices. And most of the time, I don't think about it like that.

And it doesn't seem like such a bad thing really. These guys, mostly they're nice guys, they're lonesome, away from home, they're about my age. What does it hurt? We make them a little happy, we all have a good time.

And it's easy not to think about the whole thing too much, because I got to keep busy, just to survive. I stay with Viola for a little while, watch how she handles men. She always keeps things light, she laughs, have a good time. I can tell I'm kind of in the way, so I make plans to get out of there as soon as I can.

She's a big help to me, though. She takes me to the best clubs, introduces me around. I got to say, I always got an easy way with people, and of course, I never have no problem talking to anyone, except maybe my sister.

Turns out that's a good thing in this line of work. A lot of the guys, they don't know what to do any more than I do, I mean about money, making conversation, that kind of stuff. Some of them of are just scared kids. Others, well, others you wouldn't want to meet in a dark alley, but I stay away from those bad boys. So I go out to the bars with Viola, I take home a guy here and there, and I save my money, real careful.

It don't take long before I get my own little place. I'm happy to have it, and I keep it nice and clean. I take some pride in that. When it rains, the rain makes music on the tin roof. Sometimes I like to sit and listen to that sound, other times it drive me crazy. But still, even today, if I hear rain on a tin roof, I will think back to that time and place.

First thing I do every morning is make the coffee. Then I go to the market. I get eggs and lentils and teff, which is the main thing. Teff is cheap and it's what everyone mostly eats. You can make it into a bread called *injera*. It's good for you. We eat it because it's so cheap, but I got to laugh because now, in my American life, the other day I see teff selling in the health food store for lots of money. Everyone wants it because it's high in protein and the new health food. We eat it because we couldn't afford meat.

Of course, we eat other things, too. Sometimes you might get milk and make yogurt out of it, but milk is expensive. And meat, well meat is just for special occasions. When I come back from the market I cook up my food, wash up the dishes and sleep. I sleep in the afternoons, so I can go to the bar at night and stay up late.

I do hang around a little with the other girls at the bar, but basically they are competition. You might think I'd get to be really close with the other working women, but it's not like that. I stay close to Viola because we knew each other before, and we help each other out. But I'm more careful with the other women. Yeah, we do each other favors once in a while, but we don't really talk. Maybe we're still all a little uncomfortable about what we're doing. And we're busy of course, just surviving.

So except for me and Viola we don't tell each other our problems. We are outcasts really and we keep to ourselves. No married ladies are going to invite us over to be with their families. For one thing, they don't want us around their husbands, although they don't have to worry none. But there I am.

But I find, if I don't let myself think too much during this time, it's a pretty good life I mean I got food, I got a great place and no one is yelling at me, or hooking up electric wires to my chair to shock me and laughing like my sister's kids did way back when I lived with them. I got nice clothes and nice things.

And there's something else people don't understand, really. I feel cared for. I know people will think it's just about sex, but it doesn't feel that way. Sex and love and holding each other and laughing — well they all go together. Maybe some places it's different, the men are nasty or want things they can't get anywhere else. But here, at the army base, these guys are mostly just regular American kids. It turns out Kagnew base is really a special place although I don't know it at the time.

Turns out that Eritrea was the perfect place for an American Base during the cold war because the army can listen in on secret messages from the rest of the world from where it was. That explains all those huge satellite dishes we see all the time and don't know what the heck they are.

But more to the point, the boys there are mostly the smartest kids they got in the army, guys who could wire up anything, guys who could speak lots of languages, you name it. And course they're young and sometimes homesick with no girls their own age around and no one who cares for them nearby.

So the army wants them to be happy, and they look the other way on lots of things. As long as they keep the drugs and the other stuff off the base, no one cares if there are bars, and drugs and women right outside. Kagnew base is a wild place in those days, in the 1970s.

I don't care if people say it's wrong. I had movies, dancing. The soldiers want you to like them, because they don't want you to go with anyone else. They bring you gifts, treats, things you can't get anywhere except for the stores on the base. In some ways, my dreams from when I'm a kid come true. Some nice smelling cheerful man is bringing me candies, just like I watched fathers do for their kids, and I'm loving being the center of someone's attention for the evening.

Viola has a steady guy, and lots of the girls do too. They find a guy and stay with him. I tell Viola that I want to do that too and she agrees. "Honey, you need to find nice guy to be with and take care of things, like I do," she tells me. "Ben might have a nice friend I can introduce you to. Some guy looking for someone steady."

And that's what happens. She introduces me to a guy named Ricky. I stay with him for a long time, until he's supposed to go back home. He's a sweetie, this guy. He buys me things, he takes care of things, he tells jokes, he takes me to American movies. He comes from a rich family and he hates being in the army. His family made him join because he got some girl pregnant back home. Sometimes Ricky tells funny stories about it, sometimes he cries. I know this isn't what he meant to happen in his life. And believe me, that's something I understand.

But he try to make life a little better for me. One night, I remember specially, he shows up with some flowers in one hand and the other hand was behind his back. When I took the flowers, he brought the other hand in front, and opens it up and there was a little piece of red tissue paper, tied with a pink tiny ribbon. Who knows where he even got it. And I opened it up, and there was a little pair of gold earrings, perfect for me. I put them on, and tears dripped onto my face.

He kissed them away and said, "Baby, what's the matter?"

I was ashamed to tell him I couldn't remember anyone ever just giving me something. I wrap my arms around him, and in that minute, we feel love for each other. Not love like this is forever, not love like we are going to be a family. But love, like people can be good to each other, make each other happy for a minute. Like that song line, "Help Me Make it

Through the Night," that kind of love. That night, after we have sex, we lie in each other's arms and listen to the rain on the roof of my house.

And it gets better. Viola and I move into a beautiful villa together, along with two other girls. It's big and airy, and just off the base. I got a beautiful bedroom, and we all share a living room, dining room and kitchen. This place like out of the movies it's so pretty.

CHAPTER

11

Ricky and I stay together for as long as he's there. We have fun but we both know that he will leave in a while when his time will be up. But 1 remember that time like it was a few minutes ago.

Me and Ricky, Viola and Ben we go out, we party, we have wine. I don't do drugs, but honey, I think I get high just walking from the base to our villa. Everyone is smoking marijuana and not much the army can do about it if you are not on the base.

So, like I say, you can smell the marijuana in the air, coming from all those villas around the base. And they got something called "khat" that you can chew on. Totally legal, they pass it around everywhere, the bus station, the bars. I don't know what it is, but it gives you a real nice buzz, makes you high. They also got water pipes that lots of people share.

In those months, me and Ricky, we drink, and dance and see movies. I'm living in my gorgeous villa that I have fixed up real nice and homey, and I got a television set. We watch television, and see all the "I love Lucy" reruns, and the "Three Stooges, and I laugh and laugh, even if I don't always know what they're saying. Ricky laughs too and we feel close.

Sometimes Viola and I watch television together, too, and when we do, we make up stories when we don't understand all of it, to fill in the blanks. We watch Bill Cosby and his old comedy routines. Again, we don't know what he's saying, but we don't need the words. He is funny with no words, just his sounds, and his bouncing the basketball. We love him.

When Ricky and I go out to watch Italian movies they are subtitled in English which, of course, I can't read. I understand a little English when people talk nice and slow, although at the time I think I'm a hot shot with my few phrases of English. The movies we see are mostly Italian westerns, or Indian movies, or American movies.

We love Mr. Steve McQueen. We see "Hang Them High" and we love it. And we see "Mother India." Oh, how I cry at that. Such a sad movie and I remember it so well, even today. Mother has to raise her kids alone, three sons, one bad, two good. Seem like all the movies are sad, most of the people struggling, I feel for it.

One day Ricky comes over and tells me he has his orders and he's going to be leaving in a few weeks. Of course, I knew this would be happening, but somehow, I'm not expecting it. I got so used to living in the day, not thinking ahead, that this comes as a shock. But I don't let him know. Nothing he can do anyway.

I smile, tell him we'll celebrate, go for a good dinner, great sex.

He smiles, for him, this is a happy time. He's excited about getting back to the States, seeing people he knows, getting out of the damn army.

For me, it means I got to find someone new, got to drag myself around till I get a new guy who'll treat me right. And, I don't tell him, I don't even tell myself, but I'll miss him.

We party and party until he leaves and I hug him good-bye. After he leaves, Viola try to cheer me up.

We go out to one of the bars and watch the strobe lights. The American boys love the strobe lights. I guess it's the '70s after all, and even if they are in Asmara, they are still kids, some who think about themselves as hippies not too long ago. They don't talk to us about their feelings about being in the army, about being where they are. It's only later, I realize some of them probably didn't want to be there at all, and some were just relieved they weren't in Vietnam. But then, I don't know nothing about it. They are just nice guys, wanting to enjoy life.

Me and Viola, we try to dress the part, too. I get a tie dyed shirt and a fringed vest. I have a headband and a big peace symbol that I wear around my neck. Hey, you got to get in the spirit of things. Viola and me, we follow the styles. We get a catalogue, and we have some of the other women make these things for us. We are pretty good with sewing and all, and we can copy anything.

One day Viola comes home and she all excited. "Look at this, Ghabriela." She's got a brand new *Vogue* magazine some-one give her. It's from the States and it's got all kinds of clothes in it.

She picks out one outfit and she says she loves it. We are both about the same size, so it will fit both of us. We can make it together and then share it. It sounds good to me. I can make anything. I learned to do all that kinda stuff in the orphanage and I'm good at it.

I tear the page out of the magazine and put it up on my wall. Probably not a lot of *Vogue* pictures of an evening gown hanging on the walls in Asmara, but you never know, and hey, it works. We keep it there, so I can look at it for the next few days. I got to think about where I can get the material. We ask

Viola's boyfriend, Ben, and he tells us no problem. He is as good as his word.

Two weeks later he comes over to us and he got a big smile, hands behind his back. He grins and throws the package at me.

I hurry up and open it and it's the most beautiful material I ever seen in my life. It's got some gold thread running through it and it's silky and soft.

Me and Viola make it together, we sew our pieces, we put them together, and we finish it. It's beautiful, and I know a happy feeling inside. I have something special, something wonderful, but more than that, I am connected to other people who help me.

But there are the bad times too. The times I lie in my bed alone and wonder if anyone will ever even remember I'm here. I wonder how I got to this place, the girl that had dreams of a husband and family and white picket fence and lots of kids of my own, is living near the army base just trying to survive. I don't think about it long, I try to push those thoughts from my head. Sometimes, though, when I think about it, the anger comes up in me, and I can't push it down.

During that time I talk to God and ask what the heck he thinks he's doing to my life. I know I must have a purpose, I feel it inside, but I got to survive first. I just think if I can hang on long enough, I'll find out what he has in mind for me. It might seem odd, there I am, selling myself to survive, and yet I'm thinking about God all the time. I go to church, too, all during this time. People might not think of it that way, might be surprised with what I'm doing that I still go to church, but in my own way, I'm religious during that time. I think God understands I'm having a tough time and doing my best. And when you go to church in Asmara, you feel love for human beings, you want to give more, and you feel connected to God and you listen to the priest.

Of course, I don't take communion. Here, children take communion until about age seven because they are considered not to be able to do anything wrong, knowingly, when they are that young. But after that, people don't take communion unless they are living exactly by the rules, and the rules are very strict. And of course, I'm not living by the rules, not only exactly, but at all. I make peace with that. I do what I need to to survive.

I hear someone once say that being spared is not the same as being saved. Being saved means you forgive, you don't have anger in your heart. Believe me, honey, at that time I'm not there. I got lots of anger.

I'm angry at my mother for dying, and angry at all the relatives who passed me around, and angry that no one has cared. Most of all, I'm angry at my sister. I think if she'd been nicer, if she cared, if she'd taken me in when I was sick, things might be different.

But all that anger don't do me any good. I'm sure all those people I'm so mad at must have a different story to tell, but I don't care. Once you get anger in you, it's kind of like a little sac of pus in your body. Sometimes it's walled in and you don't even notice it, but sometimes it break open and spill out and you got a fever and nothing is right any more. So I try not to think about it.

I haven't seen most of my family in ages, although Andu comes to Asmara every two years and always sees me when he visits. Now that I got money, I try to give him some, but he never wants to take it from me. But still, I manage to put money in his pockets, hide some in his jacket.

He smiles and says, "Oh, Ghabriela!" But I know he's happy to have it because money is so tight in Tagrid and he has all those kids now.

Between those visits, I think about Andu and it's enough for me to know he's in the world, letting his kindness wash over things. I don't have to see him, I just think about him. I picture him and his family living in our old town, the children helping him farm. But to go there takes a very long time, involves mules, and horses, and wading through rivers and climbing mountains and I don't do it. I just think he will be there forever.

Not long after he first tells me he's leaving, Ricky goes home. He's gone, just like that. I was lonesome, but I take happiness from doing things with Viola and pretty soon I find a new boyfriend, Jake. Jake wasn't anything like Ricky. Ricky was a gentleman, a caring person. Jake, I don't know, was kind of wild at heart. And I didn't choose him.

It wasn't like I said to my girlfriend, "Look at that fine looking soldier." No, he spotted me somewhere, and after that, he just had his eye on me. I don't know what got to him, but he was head over heels about me from the minute he saw me, and he wasn't about to let me go.

He wants me, and would say anything, do anything that he thought would work.

At first things were working out pretty good. He was crazy about me, take me everywhere. But somehow, I feel like something is not quite right. I feel like he has a mean streak, just the way he talks about things, and I know he has a crazy, jealous side. He gets upset even if he sees me talking to someone. But I push all that out of my mind and try not to think about it.

Although in some ways, he is just like the other guys I went with in the army, there's something different about him. I can't put my finger on it, exactly. Maybe it's like he's much more intense. From the beginning, there's something that makes me uncomfortable. He wants to own me. He wants to know everywhere I go, everyone I go with. But he's crazy about me. He loves me. He tells me this all the time. And he buys me things, pays for my little villa.

He is from Colorado. He grew up for part of his life on a reservation, grew up poor. Now he is a hard worker. In addition to the army, he has part time jobs that bring him more money and he likes to spend it on me. That part is okay.

I try to be nice to him, I take him dancing, I go for dinner, I tell jokes, I look pretty, I try my best. But he's so serious all the time, and I can feel his anger and his fear all the time. I got anger of my own, so in some ways I understand it, but he doesn't have the kindness I got too. Although he never hit me, I got to say that for him, he's always threatening me.

"Where were you last night, Ghabriela ? I came by and you weren't here," he says to me.

And it makes me want to be mean and say things like "What's it to you, honey? I 'm not here, I be somewhere else. None of your business."

And of course, this drives him crazy. Sometimes he tells me he'll kill me if he catches me with another man.

But pretty soon I'm distracted from these problems with Jake because of Viola. One day I come home and I see her sobbing. I ask what's wrong and she doesn't say nothing, at first.

Finally, she tells me, "Well, Ghabriela, I got lots of news. Ben's got his orders and he's shipping out in a few weeks. He's thrilled. All he's talking about is how he can't wait to get home."

"Oh, Viola," I start to comfort her, but she closes her eyes.

"It gets worse," she says. Then she tells me she's pregnant.

"Ooh," I say. Course we all do things to keep from getting pregnant. Condoms, pills, you name it. We know about them. But in this line of work, sometimes things happen.

I know there won't be any discussion about what to do, only how. Some women do have their babies, but it is hard to do, and it don't feel right to bring a kid into the world like that. And Ben is already planning his life thousands of miles from here, probably thrilled to be seeing all his old girlfriends. Viola knows this isn't real life for him, this was just something to make it through the night, ease his pain of being away from home.

Most of the women in our line of work, when they got to do something about a pregnancy use home remedies, home remedies like coat hangers. Sometimes they make visits in the night to someone who knows someone who did this for a cousin of someone. That always cost money and probably isn't much safer than the coat hanger.

Abortions are kept a private, something done quiet, like in expensive private clinics. As far as I know, wealthy women are the only ones that can afford that kind of abortion, and they don't talk about it.

I put my arms around Viola and tell her we'll work it out, I'll nurse her through. It'll be all right, I say.

She don't say nothing. She knows maybe it will be alright and maybe it won't. We both know people die from this. Also, whatever happens, she knows she's in for a lot of pain.

This is the dark side of our lives. I'm beginning to think that maybe I have to get back to that old dream of mine. Maybe I have to start thinking about tomorrow again. After all, I'm back on my feet now, healthy again after that stroke, got some money. But I know in my heart I'm still in survival mode.

CHAPTER

12

So, I don't have to tell you, what with Viola's problems, and Ricky gone and all, life feels darker right then.

One day, I'm in my villa, cleaning up. I'm starting to cook something up on the stove when I hear a knock at the door. First, I think maybe it's Jake. He's such a jealous type he's always coming around to check on me. But when I answer the door, it's my sister.

I hardly ever see my sister, although she doesn't live very far. I haven't seen her for a very long time, not since after I just got out of the hospital. So if she shows up, I know it's bad news. I start to say something kind of sarcastic to her, but when I see her face, I stop. I know right away something is really wrong.

"It's Andu," she whispers. "They sent someone from his village to come get us, quick. He's sick, very sick. He asked for us."

My heart drops like a rock. I think back to the last time I saw Andu. He got some nose bleeds, but he was okay besides that. He'd lie on the bed with his head back and then he'd be fine. He tell everyone not to worry. I hadn't seen him for a long time, though, and he was due about now to come visit me like he always did.

"What's wrong with him?" I ask her. No point asking if it's serious, because they wouldn't have sent for us if it wasn't. They got no telephones. They send some kid up, take lots of buses, lots of hours to get to us.

"Listen, Ghabriela, we all going there. We gonna take the bus, till we get to the mountains. Then we got to take a donkey up the hills. Wear stuff you can travel in. You got to be ready in about an hour. And don't dawdle around, you hear me? You meet us at the square in town, with some clothes, some food for the trip." Then she disappears.

It's not like we hug and kiss and help each other out. I sit myself down on the bed for a few minutes, and I cry. I run over to Viola's room and tell her I'm going to be away for a few days, tell her to look after things for me.

"Sure, sweetheart," she says.

"You'll be all right?" I ask.

She nods. I hate to leave her just then, but what choice do I got?

I put some things in a bag to take with me. I look around and take some food for the journey, too. Mostly bread and water.

I am just about to leave to meet my sister when I hear a knock at the door. This time it really is Jake. He's looking cheerful, but he sees the bag in my hand and his face clouds over. Really. Like dark clouds rushing in. It scares me.

He puts his hand on my hair, and says, kind of menacingly, "Where are you going, Ghabriela?"

I tell him, "My brother is sick, I got to go there quick."

He quizzes me, "Your brother? Really?"

Finally, I say to him, "Jake, I don't have time for this stuff. I got to go. It's my brother. You can believe me or not, but get out of my way."

He does, and I run to meet my sister. I'm just late enough to make her mad, to set the tone of the trip, but she only says, "Finally."

The bus is getting ready to leave, but we make it. There are five of us going — my sister, and some other friends of hers. The trip by the bus is long and hot. I sit on a seat by myself at first, but later a woman nursing a baby gets on. There are always women nursing babies in Eritrea, and you see breasts hanging out everywhere, long breasts, full breasts, skinny breasts. It don't matter to anyone. It's just the way it is.

I smile at the baby and it smiles back. I feel sad for a minute, thinking of my son. But then I push the feeling away. I got enough to worry about with my brother.

The bus trip is long, hours and hours, and hot. The windows are open to let in some air, but it lets in the dust, too. There's been a drought and everywhere, it's dry and the dirt and sand fly around.

After hours we get not too far from Andu's village. We take another bus. This time I'm sitting next to a woman bringing a chicken to market. I don't care.

When we get off the bus, we walk for miles. Finally we get to the beginning of the really rural area, and it is all mountains and twisty parts. Neighbors of my brother have come down to meet us. They've got animals to help with the trip, a donkey for sure, and I think there was a horse, or two. First we have to cross the river.

They say to get on the donkey to go across, but I'm not so sure. I decide to forget about the donkey and just wade across. The river was pretty low that day, thank God. Things were pretty dry so it was easy to cross. There'd been a drought and it was bad for the farmers. Everyone on the farms been complaining and people are starting to move to the cities. Anyway, we all crossed the stream, and me, I got my shoes wet, but I'm okay.

They got a donkey and a mule for us to ride up the mountain. I take one look at that twisting path, over steep sides, no rails, nothing and I look at that mule and I shake my head. I don't like him, he don't like me. "I'm not getting on any donkey or any mule," I tell them. No way.

They laugh at me, but I stick to my idea and I walk behind them, walk and walk all the way up the mountain, on those windy little trails. I try not to look down. Too scary.

It takes a couple of hours. All this time I'm thinking what I'm gonna tell my brother, the things I want him to know. I want him to know what his kindness mean to me. I want to tell him how I always remember how he talked to me gently after I pushed that little girl down the steps, telling me just because someone treated me that way, that's not the way I want to be, not the way I want people to think of me. I got it all planned out in my head.

But then, just as we are almost to his house, children come running to us, tears streaming from their eyes. "It's too late. Daddy's dead," they tell us. My heart sinks.

"Died yesterday," the boy say. "We bury him already." I remember that. Sunrise to sundown, no one lets dead bodies sit around.

We all go into the house. My sister cooks things for everyone, try to get things set. This is the first time I meet Andu's whole family. He used to come visit us, but we never visit them, we never see them. He has five children and they are pretty young. The oldest is about thirteen now, and the youngest is just walking. His wife is there, sobbing. This is a new wife, not the first wife who beat me. I got nothing against this one.

We stay there a few days. We cook food, look after the children, then we turn around and go home. There is nothing more we can do. The wife has family there, they will help look after her, and the oldest kid is a boy, and at thirteen, old enough to take care of the family.

We head home. Me and my sister don't bond over this none.

As I sit on the bus, I feel like I am cut inside. One more loss, one more disconnection from the world. I don't know how I'm going to go home and just take up where I'd left off. I know this sadness is going to follow me everywhere. And I start to think about Viola, start to feel desperate to talk to her.

When I get back to our villa, I walk in and I know right away something is wrong. It don't smell right in there, and I know something is going on. There are some other girls there, and Ben is in the living room looking pasty and sick.

Everyone looks at me when I walk in, and I hear someone sound relieved and say, "Oh, it's only Ghabriela."

I push into Viola's room and there's blood everywhere and she's moaning. I sit on the edge of her bed and take her hand in mine. She turns over and holds my hand, smiles a little at me.

"I couldn't wait," she says. "I didn't know when you were coming back and I didn't want to get too big. It's harder then."

I nod, so she knows I understand. I don't ask questions, I figure she'll tell me what she wants to.

"I don't think it worked, though," she says. "Nothing comes out but lots of blood."

I see a newspaper. It's covering something and it's soaked with blood.

I squeeze her hand and we sit there in the dark together for a long time. I make up some special tea for the pain, and I change her sheets and get rid of the bloody ones. I try to get a doctor, but it's not going to happen. They are not going to have nothing to do with this, and they certainly are not going to come out here.

I stay with Viola all that night. I don't sleep. Ben will be here in the morning to stay with her. He won't be leaving for another few days.

After Ben comes over, I go back to my room to try to get some sleep. I'm exhausted. I haven't slept all night, and I can't remember the last time I saw the sun come up. I can't sleep, so I finally go into the kitchen to fix some tea. Maybe settle me down some.

I'm just sitting there, my head spinning. It's hard to make sense of things, of Viola's life, of Andu's dying. I'm sipping my tea looking out the window when I see a woman standing outside my place. She's smoking a cigarette and she's not doing nothing, but I know she's got a problem. I don't know why I know she's in trouble, but somehow it's like I can feel it through my bones. Since that time, I know I feel things, know things, in some different way.

At first I don't want to do anything about her, don't want to get involved. I got enough of my own problems. But something inside me won't let me just let it go. I call to her and ask her to come in.

She's got a little boy with her, about six years old and she calls him in, too.

I sigh. My morning already is not starting off good.

I give her fruit, some bread and tea, and she starts to cry. Her boyfriend threw her out that day, and she don't know how she's gonna feed herself, or the kid. She's in big trouble.

I talk to her kindly, I give her some more food. Mostly I just sit and listen to her problems. The more I listen, the more they seep into my body. Her problems are the same as my problems, same I hear over and over.

She's got to survive, but no one in the world cares whether she does or not. She got to survive for her son. Her boyfriend only wants her as long as she makes him happy. Her parents are dead. The country don't care. Everyone is in it for themselves. She don't tell me all this. She just tells me her problems, but it's starting to come together for me. I understand in some way that even though we got to solve our problems ourselves, got to get through it all and survive, those problems are part of something bigger.

Finally I give her some money. I got some extra now, anyway. I think how people willing to give money for sex, but they don't give money just to help. I know giving her money, just to give it, makes me happy.

This woman is so grateful. She tells me she hasn't heard a kind word in so long, it makes her weep to just hear someone being nice.

She's sitting there, weeping still, when I see Ben come out of the bedroom. I take one look at his face and I know something really bad is happening. I shoo the woman and boy out of our place, pressing the fruit and money into her hand.

Ben looks pale and scared and guilty. He needs to get some more rags to soak up blood. My heart sinks. I jump up and rush into Viola's room. I know something is happening.

She is in bad pain, and is pushing and there's blood everywhere. I start to back up, to get help, to get away, when something comes out of her. I don't look real close but I can't help catching a glimpse. My stomach knots up. It's clearly dead.

I go out to see if I can find someone to help, but I can't and when I go back in her room, Ben is cleaning things up. It's gone, wrapped in a newspaper.

Ben blurts out, "Oh my God, it worked."

Viola and I look at him. I feel like to him, it's just a solution to a problem. And then he starts to cry. I don't say nothing, but I'm not moved to comfort him. In that minute I see him, I see the army, I see what I'm doing, all of it, as the problem.

Something in my heart is hardening up. I still feel like I want to give to people, but now I'm dividing people up, the good ones, the bad ones. Already I'm starting to put distance in between "them" and "us." And I got no sympathy at all for the people on my bad list. I'm beginning to see how all of this fit together. I start to see how no one cares for me and Viola, how things are set up to be convenient for the people that matter. But I don't say nothing. I just start to know in my heart that I have to change my life.

I go back to my routine. I got no choice, but things have changed. I know things are changing, I feel a darkness closing in. I'm still seeing Jake. I'm starting to think what to do about him, when he get his orders that he's being transferred back to the States.

I'm thinking it's not such a bad thing he's leaving, although there are some rumors that the whole base might be closing in a year or two. At the time, we don't really know what the base is about at all, why these Americans are here. We didn't really think about it none. We are happy the soldiers spend money here, happy to get food, get taken to lunch. Oh I know the Italians been there, the English been there.

I never think about why everyone wants a piece of Eritrea. Partly, it's because it's on the Red Sea, but it turns out there's another reason. It's the 1970s and the world is in a cold war, everyone is spying on everyone else. And Eritrea, up on a plateau, is a great place to listen to everything in the world. But right then, I'm just thinking about how my life will be when the base closes.

So in all this, I'm shocked when Jake comes over one night and tells me he wants me to come with him and marry him. No one has asked me to do that before. It's an interesting idea. I tell him I don't know about that.

"Even if you don't want to marry me, come to America. Try it, for six months," he says. "Just for six months. Then you can decide what you want to do. If you don't want to marry me, you can at least go to school there. It will be up to you."

"I don't want to marry you," I tell him.

"You don't know that," he tells me. "I can change your mind. Besides, you don't have to promise me anything, you can just try life there. You can do anything. Remember, it's America!"

Even there in Asmara we hear all the time about America, like it's some magical kingdom.

I tell him I will think about it. I don't say much one way or another. Although I don't want to marry this guy, somehow, his asking me snap me into a different place. I start to think about being married, about having a home, a family, kids.

I haven't thought about this for years, since I was in the orphanage. You wouldn't think an orphanage would be a great place to get you to think of having a family, but I was taken care of there. I had time to think, to dream. Remember all those great stories I made up about family while I was there? I always had imagination. But then, those stories just die. I have work and pain, and survival. It's all I think of, to survive. But now, suddenly, it's different.

I start to think maybe it would be nice to have someone who will care for me, maybe I can have more. I start to think in this frame of mind, when I dream of getting married, the face I see bending down to kiss me is never Jake's. It isn't anyone in particular, but it's never full of rage, of anger, like Jake's face. Even when he isn't angry, he always looks intense, always so full of, I don't know, emotion.

I don't feel calm, at peace, with him. He tells me he loves me, he can't live without me for a second. He wants to make me happy. When he brings gifts, he never brings one or two things, but a sack full. It's all too much, somehow.

Finally the day comes for him to leave and for me to make a decision. I go over to see Viola, to talk to her. She has not been well, and I worry about her, but since this whole thing, her getting pregnant, things feel different, not just between me and her, but between me and the world.

I feel that things are happening, changing now in Asmara, but it's still under the surface. People from the countryside are starting to pour into the cities. They don't look too good either. They're skinny, there's rumors of crops that are failing. There's not much work for them in the cities. And politics, so much going on. I don't follow it too much, I try to stay out of it, but you hear it all the time. There was a state of emergency and they replaced the governor of Eritrea with a general. You can feel in the air something is going to happen. You see soldiers everywhere. People whisper about insurgencies.

And people are starting to talk about politics, starting to have anger in their voices. I'm feeling like leaving wouldn't be such a bad thing. And with Andu gone, I feel like a rope that has connected me to this place has been cut, sawed off.

That night Jake comes over and he takes me out for a big dinner, we drink wine. I know I got to give him an answer. I know I been thinking all day, and I know I got to leave here. I also still want to go to the place I don't know, just like when I was a little girl, and I want to see the things I haven't seen.

Finally I tell Jake I will come, but only to try it. I'm not promising nothing about marriage. I'm only hoping in my heart that I'm not going from the lion to the leopard once more.

It turns out it was good I agree to come to the United States, because pretty soon things in that part of Africa really start to unravel.

CHAPTER

13

Jake has to leave the next day, but he tells me he will start the paperwork to send for me. I believe him. He tells me I better not be with anyone else, I better watch my step. He will have his friends look in on me.

Jake is so worried I will find someone else while he is gone that he asks his best friend Wally to take care of me. Jake sends me gifts through Wally, takes care of my apartment, does everything so I won't need to find someone else. I only met Wally a couple of times before, but now he shows up pretty regular, with letters from Jake, clothes from Jake.

This guy Wally is so different from Jake, like night and day. Where Jake has all this anger, all this emotion, Wally is nice and calm, quiet, no emotion, nothing. It's finally peaceful in my place again. Wally don't beg me for nothing. He's happy to bring me stuff from Jake. He takes me out sometimes for a quiet dinner. We talk. Wally know all kinds of languages. He's a smart man, educated. He's a very different man than Jake for sure. And he's religious. He takes his religion serious and try not to hurt anyone.

I start to really feel something for this guy. When I think of having a home, a family, I picture someone like him, quiet, calm. At the time, those qualities, they really appeal to me. He isn't the kind of guy who wants to go out and raise hell, and I'm liking that.

Gradually we start to get closer. We pretty shy with each other at first. But one evening, pretty soon before I'm going to leave for the States, we go to dinner and Wally takes my hand. Now considering the kind of work I'm in, that might not seem like a big step, but somehow, with this guy, I know it means he really, really, cares for me. He just holds my hand quietly in his for a long time. He understands me. I feel like he knows I'm in survival mode, but there's a different me underneath. I feel happy inside, understood.

I'm supposed to leave for the States. Jake has set everything up. I'm wanting to go to Jake less and less every minute.

"What should I do?" I ask Wally. We both know what I mean. We don't say much about it, but we are falling for each other.

He thinks about it. He feels I made a promise to Jake, to give things a chance for six months and I should keep that promise. He tells me he will write to me, but only to let me know how things are here. He doesn't want to interfere with things. However they go, they go, but give them a chance he says.

Que Serra, Serra, I think.

The day before I'm supposed to leave, I look around the villa. The sun is streaming in. Beautiful things are everywhere. I feel scared leaving everything I know, but I also feel excited. And I know I have to leave everything I've worked so hard for. I can't take much besides a suitcase of clothes and some of my photographs with me. I'm going to have to give away everything. I'll leave the furniture and pots and pans for Viola.

I tell Viola to take what she wants, but she doesn't take much. She doesn't have the heart for it, somehow. Then I talk to the woman with the little boy I helped out a while ago. I still keep track of her from time to time and I tell her I want her to take what she wants.

She looks over my stuff and takes all my American fashion magazines, and she takes the food I won't be taking and the clothes I won't be needing. I call in some of the other girls and they pick through the rest. Later on, my sister is mad that I don't give her everything before I go. It's another thing wrong between her and me, but I don't care.

The day I leave, I hug Wally goodbye, and step on the airplane. I never even been on an airplane before and I'm terrified, but I smile and wave, make believe I'm so happy.

But all during the flight, I know I'll be seeing Jake at the end, and I dread it. What I don't know then, won't know until much later, is that I have escaped from an almost certain death. Everything will be chaos, and the worst health crisis that the world has ever seen will be right here eventually. Millions will die, children will be orphaned. People will starve. But then, on that plane going to America, I don't know any of that. I'm just worried about how I'm gonna deal with a boyfriend I don't really want to marry.

Those first months in America were crazy for me. I feel like I'm in outer space. It was a long time ago, 1972, when I get off that plane. Years later, when I see the movie, E.T., I know what he feels like. It's like I'm on another planet and there is no one to talk to that I know.

When I get off the plane, it was a shock to me. Everything was brown and dead, it was late March, early April. I don't know anything about seasons, about trees losing their leaves or colors changing. In Asmara we only had dry/rainy season and everything is always green. I see brown dead things all over and I figure that's the way it's going to be. I never saw dead things come alive before. It is something I can't even think about in my head.

I'm in a place where I don't know anyone except Jake and I don't know what is going on around me. 1 am surprised by all the vacant land and it's so different from what I see on television. I don't speak that much English. I thought I was something when I was back in Asmara and I knew enough English to say a few good things. But here, it's all I hear, and everyone speaks so fast I can't understand them. Jake meets me at the airport and I have all these confused feelings running through me. I'm happy to see someone, anyone, familiar. But somehow, when I see his face, I have a sinking feeling in my stomach. And again, I feel a sense of dread. Jake is happy enough to see me. I think he was worried I wouldn't come so he also seems tense, like he's been wound up for a while. But we get something to eat and go to his place.

I'm not used to the food, I'm not used to the people. I'm homesick.

Jake works two jobs so he's never home. I know he's trying to earn money for us, but I hate being left alone in the apartment all day. All I can do is watch television until he comes home at eight o'clock at night. I thought America would be one big city. All I ever saw were pictures of New York, of San Francisco, beautiful places with lights and people and activity.

We are living in a little town, a rural area of Virginia. I don't have a car, and I don't drive anyway, so there's no place I can go. But I learn English through listening to "I Love Lucy." She's my role model. This must be what the typical American marriage is like, I think. What do I know? I never had no real family anyway.

I think maybe when I meet Jake's family it will be better. I picture his mom taking me around shopping, showing me cooking. I make up a whole family for myself. After all, I always dreamed of family. I think, maybe I got problems with Jake, but maybe his family will make up for it. I got them all pictured in my head, and I think of the things I'm gonna do to get along with them, be a part of them. I will cook special good foods for them. I can sew and make things. That's what's in the back of my head. I know he got a mom, a dad and a sister. I keep asking when I am going to meet them. He keep making excuses, he says soon we'll meet.

Meantime, I'm getting letters from Wally, nice polite letters that anyone can read. I get the woman next door to read the letters to me. "He's going to be coming to the States soon," she tells me. I feel my heart skip a little beat when I hear that. She asks me about Wally and I giggle a little.

"Oh my," she say. "You're in trouble, girl."

I push her, joking around. "Nah," I say. "No problem."

It's not long after that that a friend of Jake's, Paul, comes to visit him. He comes from Jake's hometown and he seems a lot like Jake. He talk like him and he's talking about all the people Jake know, about this and that. I can see Jake is looking uncomfortable, like he don't want to talk about all the people back home, especially he don't want to talk about his family. Every time Paul say something about the family, Jake changes the topic.

Finally, Paul says "It's too bad your parents are taking this so bad about Ghabriela. I mean, not to ever be able to see them again and all, it's terrible."

My mouth comes open when he says this. When he leaves, I ask Jake what's going on.

He tells me the reason I've never met his parents is that when they find out he's with an African girl, they disown him. Done. We don't want no African girl in this family, they tell him. But, he never tells me this.

I'm so mad I could spit. I don't know why after all the other things wrong between us, this is like the last straw. This is what breaks the deal for me entirely. I know I want to be a part of a family, and I know that is a big part of my dream.

After this, things go from bad to worse between us. I don't help matters none because I'm so angry, I can't be nice for a second. I feel tricked, used. Jake try to make it up with me. He brings me flowers, I throw them on the floor. The rage is just seeping out of me.

Don't matter anymore what he do, I can't get beyond it. And Jake's got his own problems. He don't like not getting his way. More I say "no" to him, madder he gets.

I'm starting to get scared of him, big time. He always tells me, "Ghabriela, I catch you fooling around with anyone, I kill you."

I believe him. But I know I have to do my time with him, wait till I figure out a way to get away from him. I'm stuck right now. I hardly speak any English, not so people here can understand me anyway. I got no money of my own, no job, no car. In Asmara it didn't matter, everything nice and close by, buses run all the time. Here, I'm in the suburbs — no buses, no nothing. I'm grounded, stuck like a starfish in the mud when the tide goes out. But I do what I can to get used to things. I watch television to learn more English and I'm beginning to understand more.

Rena, the woman who lives downstairs from us, is also home all day. Rena is married and has a little boy she takes care of. Sometimes when I see her with him, it makes me think of myself and my son, and I have a dark heavy feeling inside, but I push it down. I never told no one here about it, it's a secret, a part of me walled away from the world. It's buried so deep, sometimes I can't even get to it. I just know there's pain.

But I'm happy to have this woman for a friend. She's a little older than me and she mothers me. She takes me around from one place to another. She shows me how to do things like an American girl, how to shop, fix the kind of foods they have here. She helps me choose clothes and find the best bargains. She drives me around everywhere and she and I are feeling real friendship. I feel like I got family, someone who cares, in my life, and I would give anything for that, do anything.

She try to talk me into taking yoga because she goes to a class once a week. She probably figures I need it worse than her, because calm was not the way to describe me then.

Jake and I still fight all the time. And he makes fun of me running around all over the place with Rena.

I tell him I am thrilled to have a friend, someone who appreciates me, who cares for me.

He laughs at me, tells me that I'm blind, that she has a crush on him, she flirts with him all the time. "She spends time with you to get to me. She comes over here so much because she wants me." He whispers in my ear that she's made a pass at him and he's taken her up on it.

I don't know if it's true or not, but it doesn't matter to me. I don't really care what her intentions are, why she spends so much time with me. I just care that someone is being kind and nice, helping me out.

A memory about the orphanage flash through my head and I remember how I was willing to put a cactus needle in my eye to get the attention of the nice, caring nurse there. At heart, I haven't changed. Connection means everything to me.

But one thing is clear. Nothing is going to work out between Jake and me. We fight all the time. It's meanness that's growing between us, not good feelings.

Meanwhile, I'm still getting more and more letters from Wally. His first letters are nice cheerful letters, the kind anyone can read. But when he realizes the friend next door keeps my letters private for me, they change. Instead of those first nice polite letters, these letters are very different. He tells me how he loves me. This man who is so shy when we are together, pours out his feelings, tells everything, in letters.

I feel his gentleness, and believe me, right now, gentleness is something I really appreciate. I can't wait until I can see him. He understands me, knows what I'm going through. I don't know how he knows, but I can feel that he does. He tells me about knowing how it feels to be different, to be in a place you don't understand people.

I know I have to arrange to see him. I'm feeling love for him too, but there are things I need to know. I think about how his family will feel about me. I feel so alone now, my old feelings about having a family are coming back to me.

Luckily, Jake is going back to Colorado for a few days to try and talk to his parents, and to find a job out there, because he wants to move back there. He doesn't ask what I want. He doesn't think about it like that. He thinks what he wants, and figures I'll follow along. Just doesn't ever enter his mind to ask me, really. He just thinks that if I would do what he tells me to, it will all work out.

He doesn't understand who he's dealing with.

He tells me he will let me know where we're going to live. He will send for me if he decides to stay there, send me a bus ticket. I tell him I need to think about things, and say I want to stay where I am for a little while, at least until he gets things settled with housing and his work situation.

"Go," I tell him, "and then, I can follow you later."

I know, maybe I should just tell him that it won't ever work, but he's still so crazy jealous I'm afraid of what he'll do. I just want him to leave. I think I'll say anything to get him to go.

Jake leaves. He's gonna send for me, he's gonna do this, he's gonna do that. He is being all nice to me, mostly. But as he gets in his car, he pulls me close to him, kisses me hard, and whispers, "You better not be with anyone else or I'll kill you, Ghabriela."

I keep quiet. In my head I'm just saying to myself, "Just let him leave, go, go."

I watch the car go down the road and I start to breathe again. Every mile he puts between us gives me joy.

But now I'm really, really alone. I got no car, no job, no nothing. But Wally is getting out of the army and he writes that he will come very soon.

During that time, all I can think of is seeing Wally, having someone kind to talk to me, be with me. And I start to think about his family. I wonder what they'll be like. I wonder what they'll think of me being an African girl. When I was growing up, I start to think about color. Then, everyone I know is some shade of brown but color got my attention because even in my family, I'm the darkest. But I'm comfortable moving between worlds, between black and white.

My sister's husband was white, no one says too much about it. At the army base there is a mix of people, but you got to be careful some time about that. So I watch and I learn.

Almost the first thing I ask Wally is what his parents will think about the fact that I'm African. I ask if he's told them. I don't want to go down that road again.

Wally looks at me and smiles. He tells me about his family, that his parents are deaf, and that has made them understand the world differently than a lot of people. "You've got to understand my parents. They don't care where you are from, or what color you are, as long as you are Christian. That's what's important to them."

Well, okay, I think, *everyone got their things that are important to them. And I'm all right on that front.*

He tells his parents all about me. He tells them right away that he loves me, that he wants to marry me. I don't know how they feel, if this is a shock or not — but they tell him they are happy for him. They can't wait to meet me. They use sign language so Wally will translate, but I don't worry about that none. I know I can communicate without words when I need to.

Wally tells me they have always been a little surprised that he hasn't become a priest, but they are excited about having a daughter-in-law. He grow up in a strict Irish Catholic family and has been an altar boy. His family always thought he might become a priest because he was such a kind, gentle person, and he didn't date a lot, didn't have a wild side. And of course, he was such a quiet person, sign language being his first language.

I don't say nothing to him, but sometimes I think I'm kind of an unlikely choice for him, especially considering my occupation. I mean, here he is, a really smart guy, good education, comes from a family where religion is the most important part of their lives, you think I'm going to be his first choice of a wife?

I think about that sometime. I understand for me, what draws me to him. He's kind, gentle, and I been missing that in my life. I'm lonely and he's understanding. But he's got a family who loves him, a really high paying, good job and he wants me.

Now, looking back, I think I understand it. He likes the fact that I'm so outgoing and lively. I was a good looking girl too, and I'm sure that didn't hurt any either, but I think what he really likes is that I draw him out of his shell. And there's something more that I feel, that's hard to explain.

Wally like the old ways. They comfort him. He like the idea of a quiet life with his wife and he like the idea of taking care of me. Of course, since I was in a strange country and hardly knew the language in the beginning, I did rely on him a lot. But underneath, I was more independent than almost anyone he'd ever meet. I mean, I was on my own since I was four, and that feeling of needing to take care of myself didn't go away. I think later on, that cause problems.

So things work out. I meet Wally's parents and they love me. In the end, I marry Wally and I begin my life as a real American woman. We move far away, to New York State, where his parents live.

I enjoy taking care of the house and I was good at running it. I'd learned to do all sorts of household crafts and skills when I lived in the orphanage. I was a great cook, and seamstress and housekeeper. Plus, I'm just a naturally organized person. I can manage anything. And since I didn't have much formal schooling it wasn't like I was heading toward a power career. Plus, in addition to everything, we both liked the idea of a family.

But still, something weigh on me during that early time that we are together. I worry about Jake, that he will find me, and that he will make good on his threat and kill me.

I hear from my girlfriend back in the old apartment that he is furious when he found out that I was gone. I can believe it. But he is far away now, and I don't really think he will come all this way to find me.

So even though that stays in the back of my mind, it is still a good time for me. Wally's family loves me. And I love them. That part works out so well I feel like I'm in a dream. His family loves me because I take good care of Wally and the house, and I'm lively. They see that as a good match for their son. I try too to communicate with them, and I learn sign language.

Later when his dad gets sick, I take care of him every day. I feel finally I have people to care about, and people who care about me. I feel like my dreams of a family are taking shape, and I feel happiness growing inside of me.

I start trying to put together a life, though. I'm still lonely, too. I feel so different from the people all around me. I'm starting to hear more and more disturbing things all the time from people coming over from Africa, things about hunger, about war. It wasn't like there weren't problems before, but I feel like it's getting worse and worse. But still, my American life goes on.

14

One of the first things I do in my new American life is take English lessons. They offer them free at the local high school at night and I sign up for them. This course is really for people who come from all over, and want to take their citizenship test, so they need to learn enough English. I'm living now in New York State, not far from Albany, so there are lots of immigrants.

I'm really excited. too, because I'm so homesick in the beginning, I'm always looking for people who look like me, talk like me. When I walk into the class, it's like the U.N. there — everyone in my class is from somewhere far away. There are women wearing saris who I learn are from India, and men and women from Africa. I meet people from all over the place with all kinds of stories. And some of the other people are from Ethiopia, too.

I feel connected to these people. I know the pain of being separated from everything familiar. I watch how everyone acts that first day of class. They are all shy. They all know whatever it is they are used to doing, how they talk, how they shake hands or don't shake hands, it don't mean the same thing here in this new country. So they sit quietly, politely, waiting to take their cues from the teacher, find out how to do things here. But gradually, we warm up to each other.

There is a nun from South America and I can tell she is especially homesick, so the second night of class I bring her something special that I cook. I just want to make her feel comfortable, to have something home cooked, even if it is from the wrong country. And she smiles at me quietly, gratitude coming right out of her heart. After that, I bring in some special Ethiopian bread, and a hummus spread to go with it.

I ask the teacher if it will be okay if I offer it to everyone after the class is over and she says fine, what a good idea. The teacher is a really warm person and this helps out. I put out the food at the end and it gets all of us laughing, joking, social with each other. We might not be able to talk the same language, but hey, everyone understands eating together and sharing. After that almost every class, someone brings in something to share, so we become a pretty close group. We aren't just going there, learning English and leaving.

The nun from South America tells me she wants to introduce a girl she knows to the class. The girl is from a wealthy Ethiopian family and her name is Hannah. She is about seventeen or eighteen, and her parents sent her here to keep her safe, because of all the stuff going on in Ethiopia. Her father was a high government official, and the political situation was getting angrier and angrier, more and more dangerous each day. Her parents arrange for her to live with the nuns at the Sacred Heart Convent in Albany and she is living there, but she's lonesome and doesn't know too many people from back home.

So I decide to have a get-together at my house, invite everyone from the class and include Hannah. Some people ask if they can bring friends and I say "Sure, honey. Bring as many people as you like." That's how our weekly get-togethers start, how they grow.

Since I was the only one who was married with a home, I would try to make things comfortable for everyone, do some special things. And besides I love to cook. Every weekend I'd cook up lots of food, the smell of berbere spice and chicken watt filling the air. And sometimes I'd throw in my Italian Ethiopian specialties, like lasagna and my meatballs, and we would all get together for meals and music. Wally loved it too, but he stayed mostly on the outskirts, quietly enjoying. He was that kind of guy.

But then, one morning, one of the college students called me up. I remember it like yesterday. It was a clear September day, the leaves just starting to turn, It was a couple of years after I got here, so that would be 1974. I could hear right away, something is wrong. His voice is hoarse, he is whispering, like the words are all stuck in his throat. "Have you heard what happened?" he asks.

"I just woke up, honey," I tell him. "I just pour myself coffee. I don't know nothing."

"They overthrew the government. Haile Selassie is in jail," he whispers.

I don't know why he's whispering. I think he just can't make himself say the words. "The communists have killed thousands of people in the government. We are trying to find out who, trying to get the lists."

"Oh my," I say. I can't think of words to say at first. I am in shock. Then it comes to me. Hannah's family is all there, they are in the government, high up. I whisper too, "How is Hannah? Do you hear about her family?"

"We don't know anything yet. But it doesn't look good," he says.

"Listen, Honey," I say, "I'm going to get her. You can all come here as soon as you can."

I finish my coffee, I throw on some clothes and I drive over to the convent. I don't even call first. I know Hannah needs to be with us.

When I get there, I see she's frantic, but she is thankful that I am there. She is crying, sobbing and she runs into my arms and I just hug her. Between sobs she is saying something about how terrible this is.

Over and over she say, "What do you think happened to my parents, my brothers?"

It's like she can't stop saying it, but we don't want to think too much about what happened. We both know whatever it is, it can't be good.

I bring her back to my house. Wally, bless his soul, has put on more coffee. Word is out and slowly people start appearing at the house. This is before e-mail, and cell phones and the Internet, so news travels slowly, you just got to wait.

We heard that the papers, especially the big papers, were going to have lists of all the government officials killed, the names of people jailed, when they had them. And we waited and waited, every minute feels like an hour.

One of the men ran to town to the Lark Street News and waited for the New York Times to come in. As soon as it did, he drove back to my house with every copy he could get his hands on, maybe twenty in all. Everyone grabbed a paper and we started to go over the lists of people who had been killed. We didn't have to go very far in the lists. Hannah's parents were in the names of the first group killed.

She sat there and wept. Soon, she would have to figure out what to do. She was in the expensive dorm at Sacred Heart. There would be no more money either. No family, no money, no nothing. Her world turned upside down that day.

There is nothing to do. We sit there in shock, I keep bringing out coffee and food, and everyone is looking at the lists, and some of the students are going down to the newspaper store and bringing in more and more newspapers. Everyone is upset.

But even in that upset, some people hope some good will come out of this. They hope that at least maybe the communists will make it better. For a very long time, things in Ethiopia had been very uneven, with many, many poor, hungry, and sick people, and a few very rich people. So maybe a new government will change things. Me, I didn't think that things would change. I think people are people and I don't think the new ones are gonna make things any better than the old ones did. I been looking around for a long time, and I don't see a lot of help for poor people. I understand how things work.

We can't do nothing anyway. We sit there all morning in shock with each other.

After that day, I am numb. I try to go back to my normal life. I'm gradually putting together my new American life. I got a job now, working at a food plant. I love my job. Wally thinks I'm crazy to work when we don't need the money, but me, I got to be doing something every minute. No point sitting around thinking about the past. And I'm starting to meet new people now, make new friends, American friends.

People appreciate me at the plant. I'm always cheerful, I work hard, and I try and dress nice, take care of myself, so I look pretty good, too. They love me there and I like getting out every morning, having something to do, someplace to go.

I'm also trying to get pregnant and I'm dreaming of having my nice little family. I still got those Rock Hudson-Doris Day movie scenes in my head from those trips to the movies long ago in Asmara, and I got something to compare my life to, and it's not looking so bad. Really all I need is the picket fence — and the kids.

The pregnant part isn't happening. First I just shrug it off. Some things need time. *Que Serra, Serra.*

But even though I'm trying to live my nice little life, I keep hearing new things out of Asmara and out of Ethiopia, and each one is scarier than the last one. It don't take long to see, not too many people gonna be better off now that the communists take over. Every time I get together with the people from that part of the world, seems like all we can talk about is war.

We hear about all the killing, and we hear about the communists taking away all the private property. The system has changed, and now no one can own much private property. No one can have more than the house they live in, and it better be small, although sometimes if you got no other income, you can keep a small rental house. Things change now. Any government official can come into your house at any time to inspect things. They don't have to tell you who accuse you.

That's what I'm hearing anyway. I think about all the people I knew back in Africa and worry about them creep in. I try to push it from my mind, nothing I can do anyway.

My friends tell me there is a whole community of Ethiopians in New York City now, people who have escaped from there. One day, my friends and 1 take the train there to check things out.

I see people in the street fairs selling things, beautiful things. Mostly they sell fabrics, and I ask about them. The area around where my old village used to be is becoming industrialized, they tell me. There are all kinds of things coming out of there. And some of these people are making fiber art themselves.

But I notice kind of a difference. People ask me where I'm from, where I was born. The people from Ethiopia are loyal to Ethiopia and angry with Eritreans. They hate Eritreans. The Eritreans don't like the Ethiopians, don't like that I was born in Ethiopia. It's so strange because I was born in what's now Ethiopia, grew up in Eritrea, and it was all one thing. I don't make no difference between them in my mind. But now I know I have to be careful what I say. But I don't want to get involved in politics. I just want to get along.

I try still to connect with the Ethiopians I meet. One afternoon I get a phone call from a lady I know from church.

"Ghabriela," she say, I have a young man here with me, from Ethiopia and he's going to college here. Things have gotten so bad, he can't go home for the holidays, and he's run out of money period. He needs a place to stay."

"Sure, honey. Bring him over," I say. Right away, I start making some nice food, I grind some coffee beans, set up the coffee, and everything smells so nice.

This lady brings over Solomon. He has a big beautiful smile like Andu had but his energy is totally different, not calm.

I put out my hand, and he grabs it between his hands and tells me how nice it is to meet me, how he is here all alone, but how he gonna do wonderful things.

I don't know, but people who tell me how they gonna do wonderful things make me take a step back. But I welcome him in and he drinks my coffee and eats my food and tells me how grateful he is.

He moves in a couple of weeks later and he's okay. He cleans up after himself, he helps me with the dishes, something that shocks me. I don't see a lot of African men running over to help with dishes, believe me. I don't see a lot of American men do that either, come to think of it. But anyway, it goes all right.

Pretty soon, though, I start to see mail come for him from all over, from strange organizations. And I see all these pamphlets in his room, fists raised, revolution on them, for sure. And he starts getting lots of phone calls. I can see he's involved in politics up to his neck.

I ask him about it. "Solomon, what's going on here? I thought you're here to study, finish your school. I don't see you working none on classes. I don't see you going to school," I say gently.

He sits down on the edge of the sofa and motions me to sit too. He takes my hand in his and tells me about the corruption all around me. He tells me he can't just study when there's so much to do to right the wrongs of the world. He tells me that revolution is needed.

I look at him long and hard. Some ways I understand what he means. I know in my heart that things in the world are wrong.

"Believe me, honey, I felt what you're feeling," I tell him. "But this is not my way. I don't want to be involved in revolution, in murder, in bloodshed. I give you a place to stay to study, not to organize revolution."

He looks at me, "You don't understand, do you?"

"I understand more than you think," I say. Eventually, I ask him to leave, and he does.

Somehow dealing with my people from my part of the world is getting very complicated. I am trying hard to stay out of any politics, but politics is running down the street after me. I'm trying as hard as I can to put in some distance.

Besides, something in me is changing. I'm thinking I can leave all this behind, all the anger, all the war, all the poverty and all the hurt. Gradually, I'm moving away from it, gradually I'm moving more and more into my new life.

I had brought a box of pictures from Ethiopia and I kept it under my bed, but I don't look at it no more for comfort. I don't look at it no more at all. Sometimes, I kick a little corner of it, shove it a little further under the bed when I'm making the bed up, cleaning, something like that. I don't want to think of those things. I'm not that person anymore, I'm a new person, a different person. I have other things on my mind. I want a family now, now that I got a husband and a house, and a job. I'm not just in survival mode, anymore. I can afford to have a few dreams.

One day a friend comes in and says, "Ghabriela, sit down. I heard some bad news from Ethiopia."

"I don't got to be sitting down to hear bad news from Ethiopia. All the news from Ethiopia is bad news," I say. But I listen.

She says softly, "I heard that your brother Andu's house was burned down. Either the communists burned it down or the rebels. We don't know. Guess it don't matter none anyway. They were all killed, except one, we think. Seven of Andu's children died in the fire when the village was burned. One of Andu's sons survived. He's with your sister, Gelila, in Asmara."

I sit quietly, in shock. There is full-scale war between the rebels and the communists and everyone is caught between the lion and leopard. The communists have burned down the village where I was born, where Andu's family still lived. Or maybe the rebels did it. What difference does it make? The people there, they are sandwiched in between two enemies. You talk to the communists, the rebels kill you, or you talk to the rebels, the communists kill you. You don't talk to either, they both try to kill you.

A certain kind of grief takes me over. I don't want to be a part of this, I think. I want my new life; I want to be Ghabriela, an American Girl. I don't know, maybe its anger because I can't do anything. I'm helpless. Maybe I just can't deal with all this past. I want to move on. I feel it strongly.

That night as I go to arrange the sheets on my bed for sleep, I accidentally kick that picture box under the bed. It turns out I can't sleep. Anyway, I toss and turn and somehow it bothers me that that box is there.

I get up in the middle of the night and look over at Wally. He's still sleeping. I take the box into the living room and start a fire in the fireplace. One by one, I burn all the pictures. I just want that part of my life over, gone.

I go back to sleep, but still I toss and turn. The pictures are still in my head. And worse, the feelings that go with all those terrible times are still in my heart.

CHAPTER

15

I'm getting settled in my own life. My English is getting better and better, and I'm working hard to get my American Citizenship and make my American life. I put my Ethiopian life behind me. I'm really, really wanting children now, and I'm still not getting pregnant. I'm still young enough, shouldn't be a problem.

Wally and I do all of the things people do to find out why. We visit doctors, we go to fertility clinics, I take my temperature, we schedule sex. It's not working, nothing happening. But meantime, I'm still busy with my life.

Some friends who know how bad I want children ask me, why don't you adopt from Korea?

I look at them and think about it. I'm not so sure. "I'm black, my husband white, we gonna have Asian kids? Everyone will be confused," I say, with a laugh. But I think about it.

Then, one day, out of the blue, I get a call from my niece, Genet, my sister Gelila's daughter.

Genet is just a few years younger than me, and she is the one who used to follow me around, who I took care of. I always feel affection for Genet but I'm not expecting to hear anything. I have cut my ties with Africa, burned my box of pictures. I'm living my brand new life with my American citizen certificate in my dresser drawer, my job, my new English skills and my husband.

But even before I get the call from Genet, I know I'm not done with Africa and it's not done with me. Sometimes I'm just puttering around my house, dusting the furniture, humming a tune, and something from Asmara come rushing into my head. Sometimes it's anger, rage, the feelings I had as a kid, the feelings about being mistreated. And sometimes, it's a longing, the smell of the food I used to love, the meatballs I used to taste. So it's clear that I may want nothing to do with Ethiopia, with my childhood, but it's there inside of me.

I haven't heard from anyone in my family in years, and somehow, I feel it's better to keep it that way. Every time my sister and I are in contact, I have a stomach ache. Maybe she do too, but I don't know. Her stomach ache isn't my problem. But I do have a warm spot in my heart for Genet. She was kind of like a little sister to me, so I listen. But it's so strange, her phone call just comes out of nowhere, the blue air. I was cooking when the phone rang, not expecting nothing different in this day.

Genet tells me things are terrible in Ethiopia and in Eritrea which I already know. "Oh, but you wouldn't believe how awful it all was, Ghabriela," she say. "And they took everything from Mom. You know how she survived all those years on those little income houses, the ones she and grandma fought over for years? Well the communists say no one needs more than one house and they take away anything you don't need."

I sort of laugh a little, inside anyway. It's kind of funny how that all worked out. Before Gelila's husband died, he had three extra houses that he and Gelila rented for an income. When he died, his mother claimed they were hers, Gelila claimed they belonged to her and she needed them for income. Back and forth they went, yelling, screaming, going to court. Now, the communists swooped in and took them all away. No one needs more than one house to live in they tell her. So all that aggravation between a widow and a grieving mother over the dead son's property comes to nothing in the end. I know there's a lesson there.

"We had to get out of there, Ghabriela. We were lucky we could leave. If the communists don't kill you, the rebels will." Then she lowers her voice, "Did you hear about Andu's family?" she ask.

"I heard," I tell her, and we both share a minute of quiet together. No one says anything.

"We were lucky, we got out," she says. "One of Andu's sons escaped, he went to live with Mom. The police wanted him."

"Oh," I say. Then it occurs to me, I got no idea where in the world she is. "Where are you?" I ask.

"I'm in Chicago now."

"You're here, in the States? Imagine that! How did you wind up here?" I ask in amazement.

"God must have wanted it that way. We go first to Italy, then we wind up here. It's a good thing, too." she says. "Anyway, it's a long story and it doesn't matter. But here's what I want you to know. Not everyone is so lucky to get out as you and me, Ghabriela. We hear from back home people are stuck there, they're desperate. We got friends and family who know they'll never ever be able to leave, but people are trying to get their children out, just to save their lives," she says.

"I know," I say. "I keep hearing stories. The stories get worse and worse each day," I say. I don't tell her I keep trying to close my ears to those stories but I hear them anyway. I'm beginning to wonder where all this is going. Like I say, I can never seem to get away from Africa because it come and grab me by the throat every time I move away a little. I don't have to wait long to find out why Genet is calling, what she wants.

Genet clears her throat. "You know," she says, "There's nothing left, no food, no peace, no nothing and as I say, everyone who can is trying to get their kids out of there. Your name came up, Ghabriela."

Now this surprises me. "My name?" I say, shocked. "Couldn't be good," I add with a laugh.

I can't think of any way my name came up and people at home say nice wonderful things. Me and my sister, we haven't healed anything yet. She still mad at me and I'm still mad at her.

"Actually it was good. We think about a way for everyone to benefit. We been trying to figure out who could help out and take some kids out of there. Andu's son, the one still alive, says, 'Ghabriela, she don't got no kids.' You still don't have no kids do you, Ghabriela?"

"No," I say, quietly.

"Well, in the family they say it would be perfect if you took a kid. Since everyone wants to have their kids adopted and you don't have no kids, you would be the perfect person to adopt one or two. Ghabriela, I'm sure this idea comes as a shock to you, and I know we haven't talked for so long, but I do think of you. And I don't know no other way to say it."

I sat down on my bed. It is like the suggestion comes from God. It's like God is going to give this kid to me.

I think this is a perfect solution. I will be doing something good for someone, will be saving the kid's life, and it will be from my family, be connected to me by blood. I like that.

I say to Genet, careful-like, "So, you got any special kid in mind?"

She sighs, "Ghabriela, things so bad, you got a choice. A few different kids we got in mind, all relatives. Listen, think about it, you willing to do this, we'll talk about which kid."

I tell her I will think about this. But I already know the answer in my heart.

"And, Ghabriela," she says, and pauses.

"Yes?" I ask her,

"I do miss you," she says.

I hang up the phone feeling some sense of peace in my life, like I know some pieces are going to go together. And also, maybe suffering has some purpose.

I get off the phone and say to Wally, "Wally, I got an idea."

So that is the beginning of a whole new part of my life. Suddenly things shift, suddenly, I can be on the giving end of things.

Wally don't give me no problems about this. When I tell him I got a great idea for our life, he just gives me a "I know I'm into something now" look. But Wally is always willing to listen, I give that to him. Of course, he hardly ever talks, so that gives him lots of time to listen. And he does.

When I tell him I got the answer to our kid problem, we'll adopt from Asmara, he's not shocked. He thinks about it a few minutes, kind of rolls the idea around. He likes it, he says. He has a traditional view of family, though, and he tells me, "If you want to do this, it's fine with me. But you will be the one with most of the responsibility."

Maybe this is not exactly what I want to hear, but, it's good enough for me. Course I'd rather he tell me nothing in the world could keep him from wanting to do this, it was meant to be. But it's good enough, it's the go ahead.

I sit down and think about this, and I pray to God. I feel like God meant this to be. It is like the whole circle of life.

Later in my life, one of my daughters will say to me, "If you had already had children you probably would never have thought of us, adopted us. It's good you never had children before."

I don't like to think of it this way, but maybe it's true. It must be meant to be this way, is the way I think about it. It is my way to give back to life.

I call Genet back the very next day. "I been thinking about your idea all night, all day. I'm so excited I can't sleep none. I want to adopt. You just tell me which kid," I tell her.

I hear relief in her voice, picture her body relaxing when she says, "Oh, Ghabriela, I'm so glad. You don't know what this will mean to the family. We all so worried all the time. There's no food, kids everywhere hungry, crying."

I been hearing about the problem with the food, the communists, all that kind of thing. I know people are starving, everyone is caught up in the drought, in civil war, all kinds of bad things happening. Right now, I'm thinking about the kids.

I tell Genet, "You find the kid, the right kid who needs me. I will take any kid from Ethiopia or Eritrea," I tell her.

"Thank you, Ghabriela, and God bless you." she says.

It isn't often my family has nothing but good to say about me, so I enjoy the feeling. When I hang up, I know in my heart it is the right thing to do, what I was meant to do. And I will talk to them all again, soon.

But, I should tell you about adoption in Ethiopia because the idea there is very different from adoption in the United States. They don't really call it adoption the same way, and there is no paperwork. It's usually just family to family. Someone gives a person in their family a child. That someone says, "I can't raise this kid. The child will be better off in your house," and they leave the child there, and the family takes care of it. Then no one talks about it anymore.

The person raising the kid is called Mamma, or Poppa. The birth parent comes around and visits, and is called Auntie. No one tells the kid nothing. Sometimes this works out pretty good, sometimes not.

I had a friend who didn't find out his parents weren't who he thought they were till he was an adult and he was very angry, really angry. He went back to find out the whole story and what he found was that this guy, his birth father, was married with lots of kids, and his wife had died. Then he remarried and the second woman had lots of kids. They give a boy and girl from first lady, a sister and brother, to another woman to raise. My friend was that boy, but he don't know nothing about it. He and his sister called the woman who raised him "Mom," and when the dad visited, they called him "Uncle" and he never said who he was.

The father got ill. On his death bed he told the boy about it, and the boy was so mad that he joined the army, and he was killed in a war.

The sister, who grew up with him, was crazy with grief, and the adoptive mom was angry with the father. She felt he should have asked her. So even in this simple culture, things get complicated. That's my point.

But I know if I adopt, it will be the American idea of adoption. It will involve paperwork and legal things, and I will become the mother forever. This won't be some temporary thing, getting the kids out of harm's way for a few years.

I have to think in that moment how I feel about a lot of things. In my part of Africa, everyone always have ideas about child raising, and forgive me for saying this, but no one knows what they're talking about. If you raise a kid for someone else and the kid goes bad, people tell you it's in the blood, you couldn't change nothing.

If you raise a kid you give birth to and it go wrong, everyone says it's nutrition or upbringing. No one knows. I think all this stuff is just old wives tales anyway. I think you just do the best you can.

Somewhere too, in the back of my head, I know I think the kids will be grateful they escaped all these terrible things. They will appreciate all they got and want to do the same for others, want to give the way I want to give. I don't take into account in my thoughts they will have never lived in an orphanage, never been hungry, never been beaten. They won't know all the things I will have saved them from. In my head, I don't think about the ways that suffering changes you, strengthens you. I'm just thinking the kids will think about the world like I do. They will be just like me, but not have all that anger inside. That's what I think then.

But even more than that, I don't understand all the fuss everyone makes about raising children in the first place. I hear people at work complaining, groaning, going on and on, saying, "Oh, it's so hard to raise children, so many things to think about, so much work."

I've got no patience for those people. I think they are nuts. "How hard can it be to raise a couple of kids?" I ask.

When I hear people complaining, I say to myself, *What can they be thinking?* I know I'm never afraid of hard work and I think it will be easy to take care of a kid or two and raise them. I never for a second think about the fact that I never had a mother or a family. I got nothing to look to; I will have to figure it out step by step. It never occurs to me.

CHAPTER

16

So there I am, feeling like this is something from heaven and I just have to wait, it's the way it's written. You know, I never thought anything would stop the adoption, I never think any problems will come. I think I just got to be patient and wait to hear what kid they think I should get.

It's hard to be patient, too, because now I am finally seeing my dreams about to come true. I got a husband with a good job, a nice house. I can't get pregnant but I see another way through. I'm thrilled, but it's hard to wait.

I tell everyone at work about my plan to adopt and everyone is excited for me. We're all revved to fever pitch and I feel like I'm sitting on pins and needles waiting for that call.

Finally, I get a call from Genet. She has a few possibilities, but the one who breaks everyone's heart is a relative of ours. My sister Lula, the sister I didn't choose to live with, has a daughter, a daughter, Muna, a little younger than me who already have seven children. This woman have two sets of twins, Genet tells me. Can you imagine — this poor woman has given birth to four children in just two years? She had three older children, then two years ago, she had twins. And then just a few months ago, she had another set of twins. Two sets of twins in two years in a country where no one can even feed themselves is too much for anyone to deal with. They got no food, no money, seven kids altogether and the mother isn't feeling so good. She's weak from all those kids, and from malnutrition. Her husband isn't too well but he's trying to bring in some money.

This is what Genet tells me, and we both stay silent for a minute. We both know those twins won't survive there.

I start making calls and find out I got to have the children's family apply in Eritrea to give me guardianship and I got to have a home study done here. I call up Catholic Family Services to have a social worker come out and see that I got a nice house, plenty of room for kids, a back yard.

I always keep my house spotless, always good-smelling stuff cooking in the oven, so I don't even have to get ready or pretend. I really do have a place all ready for a family.

The social worker comes out and she talks to me and Wally. Wally has a great high-paying job in civil service. I work for General Foods. I don't have to work. Wally makes plenty of money, but I like to work, I tell the social worker. I get a good feeling being with people all day, kidding around, looking good and being appreciated. And I get to practice my English. But as soon as I get the kids, I'll quit, I say.

"You don't have to do that," she tells me. "It isn't a requirement."

But I want to, I think to myself. All my life I want a family, I want a house, this dream. Now I got it, I'm gonna take time away from it? No way.

She asks how Wally and I met. That's when I smile and tell her about how I used to help out at the USO club in Eritrea when Wally was in the service. We met there, when I'm working, entertaining the troops, I tell her. "We fall in love," I add.

"That's nice," she says.

I nod.

So after my home study is finished I file some paperwork that has to go through the Ethiopian courts. It goes through, no problem. Then I fill out all the papers for the U.S. Immigration Services. I figure it will also be no problem. These kids are my relatives, they gonna die if they stay where they are. Their parents give consent for me to adopt. I want to adopt.

Then comes the shocker.

I hit a brick wall with Immigration Services. They say "no" just like that. To be adopted internationally, the kid has to meet the definition of an orphan. These kids are not orphans. They got two living parents, the parents have not abandoned them. They are living with them.

I can't believe it. I feel like I got the kids in my hand and someone grab them away.

Wally and I talk about what to do and Wally says, "Maybe it wasn't meant to be."

I tell him it was meant to be all right and I'm sure as heck not going to let these people get in the way of God's plan.

Wally looks at me, first maybe a little shocked, but knowing how I am when I make up my mind, he don't say nothing.

We hire an immigration lawyer. He doesn't do much, files a few papers. He tells me it's no use, these kids won't qualify on the orphan petition that you have to file.

I hit the ceiling. I yell at him, I shove the papers around on the desk.

Finally, I go home and I wander around my house, just kind of pacing. I can't believe it. I don't know what to do with myself. I'm so upset.

I pace, I clean, I rant.

Poor Wally has to listen to it all.

Eventually, I get tired of just telling Wally how frustrated I am, and I feel like I got to tell someone else about it.

To this day, I don't know how I came to think about it, but I decided if I'm gonna talk to someone about it, might as well be someone who might be able to do some good. I call the newspaper, the Gazette. I wind up talking to some nice reporter who I don't know from anywhere.

I am beside myself and I don't watch what I say. I'm swearing, telling her these people at the immigration department don't know nothing. I go on and on. Thankfully, I don't even remember what I say.

I can hear her pen scribbling — she's taking notes. I think maybe she'll call back some time and follow up on it. Maybe by then I'll be calmer, not sound like a lunatic.

The next day, I'm still trying to kind of calm myself down, just doing some cooking, just little things, kind of fiddling around the house when my phone rings.

My friend tells me she's calling to let me know that she saw the article and it's wonderful.

What article? I think. I'm shocked. Turns out that reporter wrote an article about me.

I don't even remember everything I say, but I know I was really mad when I was telling her.

I tell my friend, "Read the article to me." Then I say, "No, don't read it. I don't want to hear it. Oh, my God, the things I said," I tell her.

"No, Ghabriela, it's really great. You'll like it," she says. And she reads it to me over the phone.

The whole time I'm holding my breath. I can hardly listen, I'm so worried what she's gonna say, if she's gonna quote all those awful things I said about immigration.

But no, she wrote a really nice article. She told how I wanted to adopt sick, dying babies in Africa and how I couldn't because of rules that didn't make sense and red tape and all that kind of thing. It was great.

I hung up the phone, happy. Soon as I hang it up, it rings again. All morning long, it was like that, never stop. People from all over call me, some I didn't even know. The article started something. But still, nothing is happening, I'm still stuck with immigration.

Finally, I wait as long as I can, days, weeks, I don't know, and I call my lawyer again. "Nothing I can do for you, Ghabriela. You know, you could try calling your congressman."

"Really?"

"Sure," he says, "They're there to help with this kind of stuff."

Oh, I think, *America is a great country.* Right away, after I hang up with the lawyer, I call my congressman, Congressman Solomon. Turns out that was the best thing I could have done. That was when some things started to happen, just a little bit at first.

I talk to one of his assistants and I tell her how angry I am. I didn't think I'd get the kids. I tell her I want Americans to hear what the government is doing to innocent people who just want to help in a tragic situation.

She says she will get back to me, and I figure that's that, that's the last time I will hear from her.

But no, she calls right back. She says bring your paperwork over and someone else will call you later. I bring the paperwork to the office and drop it off, and sure enough, just a little while later, a man calls me. He's also from my congressman's office. He tells me he has gone over all the papers. The problem, he explains, is that according to the law, the children don't meet the qualifications of being orphans. Same thing immigration told me before.

"I'm sorry, but it's not within the law. Either they have to be orphaned, have no living parents, or be abandoned by their parents, or you would have to have lived for two years outside the country with them. That's how the law is now. You'd have to have the law changed for it to be legal."

I say, "Well, I think the law is wrong. These kids are gonna die if no one helps them, and that's that. I just want to help."

He tells me Congressman Solomon will work on it some more, and even though he doesn't give me much hope, he says he will try.

And, it turns out in a way I'm in luck because my congressman happens to be a member of the foreign affairs committee of the House of Representatives and Africa is his area of specialty. That for sure is not going to hurt, believe me.

"I understand your frustration," the assistant says sympathetically. "We are frustrated with the situation, too." Then he thinks for a minute and says, "You know, sometimes when the public gets involved. . . ."

He doesn't say any more. He doesn't need to.

Since the story came out in the Gazette, all these other papers been calling. I know it will help to tell them my story now, about how these babies in Ethiopia, my own nieces, are gonna die because of all the red tape.

A teacher at a local school hears the story and she has all her fifth graders write letters to their congressman asking him to save the babies. It becomes a project. It was bigger than the "Save the Whale" campaign, or the kid who get stuck in a well. Everyone is getting into the act.

Articles start to show up in the newspapers. The headlines read: "Couple Struggles to Bring Home Ethiopian Twins" or "Two Lives in Jeopardy" and even "Childless Couple Wants to Save Starving Twins from Horrors of Ethiopia." One writer even get so carried away she wrote the twins have already in their short lives been visited by three of the four riders of the apocalypse. I'm not kidding, she even names them: famine, war and pestilence. I guess she is right, really.

And, of course, the letters from the fifth graders at Geyser School in Saratoga Springs show up in all the local newspapers, too. The titles go something like this: "Let Ethiopian Twins be Aadopted — Don't Let Them Die" and "Ethiopian Twins Have Right to Live, Too" all written by the school children pleading with the government.

Well you can imagine how it is all looking. People are starting to flip through the newspaper pages to see how I'm doing in my fight to get the twins even before they read "Dear Abby."

But still, the INS says "no." Their hands are tied. They all want to let the twins come here.

I bet the guy whose name is on the refusal letter the newspaper printed really wants them to come here, but it's not legal. What can they do? Apparently nothing.

And what can I do? This has been going on for almost eight months now. I can't eat, I can't sleep. Wally is trying to be calming, but there's not much he can do, either.

Finally, I decide enough is enough, it isn't going to happen. I got to go to Ethiopia, just to talk to the family. They done everything at their end to get the kids over here. But I can't make it happen. I don't want to tell them in a letter or a phone call. I want to tell them in person how sorry I am.

CHAPTER

17

I make all the arrangements to go to Ethiopia and then on to Eritrea. I will go to Lula's family, who live in Eritrea, and tell them I'm not allowed to adopt the kids. I got tears in my eyes just thinking about it. I've come to think of the twins as mine. Giving them up is not something I can do easily. My heart is breaking.

I tell everyone at my job I need to go to the twins in Africa. I tell them I'm not going to be able to adopt the twins, but I have to say goodbye. I cry when I tell them, they cry when I tell them, everyone cry. But, at least I will go there, I say. I will do the right thing. Then, I'll come back to my job.

If, by some miracle, I get the kids, I won't come back to work, but I'm not expecting to get the kids. I figure I will just tell their mother what is happening or not happening. In the meantime, of course, the newspapers are still carrying the stories, the school kids are still writing letters.

Now the newspaper is writing about how after ten months of frustration, bureaucracy, red tape, I'm going to go over there and see the twins, see if there is anything I can do. Headlines read something like, "Wife Goes to Famine-ravaged Nation to Try to Bring Twins Back Alive."

I get on the plane set to go to Ethiopia. The civil war between Ethiopia and Eritrea is getting worse and worse and Eritrea is off limits to Americans. "Too dangerous," the government tells everyone.

I think to myself, *Sure they're ready to let my twins stay there, two defenseless kids, but they won't let adults who got a choice to make up their own mind.* That's how I'm thinking about it then. I have to fly into Addis Ababa, which is in Ethiopia, and where the embassy is. But the twins are in Eritrea and I will have to get there too. Don't matter to me if I'm not supposed to go there.

I fly into Ethiopia, where I am allowed to go. When my plane sets down in Addis Ababa, there is a Russian Jumbo Jet set to go to Eritrea. The officials are supposed to tell any Americans that the government won't be responsible for them if they go into Eritrea, but no one stops me, no one says anything. It's like they are blinded, don't see me. I just get on the plane.

Sometimes I think it's a miracle that lets me pass into Eritrea. Sometimes I think it's only because I lived there so long, I look and sound like I belong there. I speak Tigrinya, it's true, and that don't hurt neither, believe me. I don't know, maybe they just don't care.

I get off the plane and go to the big hotel in Asmara. There is really only one hotel for foreigners now, and it turns out that at that very moment there are all these official-looking communists there. There is some big commotion going on, a funeral for some communist leader I think, and the army brass are all there.

I settle down in my room, look out the window. Here I am, just me and the communist army brass in the middle of a civil war. And here, in the hotel everything is nice, comfortable.

It's very strange, but no stranger, I guess, than the rest of the things going on. Being here is okay. It feels right to me. What doesn't feel right is that I'm not here to get the kids. No, that doesn't feel right to me at all. Matter of fact, that feels like defeat, and one thing about me, we all know, is I don't give up easily. But for right now, there's nothing I can do, so I try to blend in, look like I'm just going about my business. Just another American citizen staying at a hotel in Eritrea during a war.

I call our embassy at Addis Ababa and say, "Here I am, in Asmara," just to let them know.

They are shocked. "You're not supposed to be there. They are supposed to warn you it's off limits," they tell me.

"No one warn me, no one tell me anything," I tell the embassy people. "I don't know nothing."

The American embassy is very upset, nervous that I am there in Eritrea. They are upset that no one called them about this, but they are not mad at me — I am just a poor citizen who doesn't know anything.

They try to talk sense to me, start with voices smooth as honey, try and coax me to go back. No one wants an international incident.

"There's a civil war going on there," they tell me, as though I don't know. Pretty soon their voices quaver a little, like they holding back from yelling at me.

There's a lot a I want to tell them. I want to tell them about the babies. I want to tell them what an awful sad task I got to tell this family about how I won't be going home with no sick babies when all of us know how these babies will surely die. And I want to tell them about the congressman trying to help and about all the school children writing letters. But all that will have to wait until I get back to the embassy in Ethiopia, in Addis Ababa. Right now, no one wants to say anything much over the telephone lines, which we all know are tapped. The embassy just wants to make sure I'm alive, I think.

In the back of mind I know I haven't really given up, yet. In the back of my mind I know these people are going to hear more of my story. But right then, I got this feeling inside that I got to get over to the family. They know I'm here now, and believe it or not, they have somehow borrowed a car, and they going to pick me up at the hotel. My visa is good for only a short time, and I am going to make the most of it.

Muna's husband, the children's father, and his friend come and get me. They got some old car, looks like it has been caught between the communists and rebels itself, and has had a hard life.

I laugh when I see that car, all the dents and dings, paint coming off, but still shined up, like they done the best they could. And I'm happy to have a way to get to the children's house fast. I feel like I'm bursting out of my skin to see the kids, although in another way I dread seeing everyone. I got to give them this bad news and I can't stand it.

But as we drive through the city, I'm not prepared for what I see. It's unbelievable. Things have gotten much worse than I remember them. People are sitting around the streets, eyes empty, stomachs bloated, no food. We get to the house and Muna and the kids are there. Everyone runs and hugs me. They don't know yet I'm here with bad news.

And I see the children, the twins, Temnit and Arseima. They look worse than I imagined. I take a good look at them. I can hear they having problems breathing, they both got bronchitis. And their stomachs are swollen. I can tell they are starving.

One of the babies is screaming and I look in her mouth. She got blisters all over her tongue. The other one is too weak to cry.

I turn away from them, from the family because I don't want them to see my tears. I don't want to embarrass the family. Pride is very important here.

I ask the mom what she is feeding them. I know she is trying to wean them because she thinks I'm taking them back, and because she got no strength herself, and hardly any milk.

I been sending her some money for baby food. Turns out there is no real baby food here, the only stuff you can buy is some powder you mix up with water. Don't seem to be doing a very good job either. It make me angry, but I know I got to focus. Anyway, no one else has food, either, and I see the adults look almost as bad.

I tell the family I will try to go down and buy some food for everyone. They tell me they will come help. I don't understand at first, but then I see what they mean. You got to stand in long lines to buy anything. But after you wait two, three hours, you can only buy one type of food, say bread. You want to buy sugar, you got to go to another line, and wait all over again. But when my relatives come, we all become line standers.

I can see some people spending their life on lines. And when you get the food, it's dirty, terrible. The bread has dirt in it, the sugar is syrupy, the milk only powder you got to mix, nothing fresh.

I want to cry every minute I'm there to see all the suffering, to see what that beautiful town of Asmara looks like now. And worse, every time I look at the twins they look so sick, I know in my heart they will die if I leave them here. I can't do it.

I begin to form all kinds of wild plans in my mind. I think I will run away with them to the Sudan if immigration won't let me bring them to the United States, that kind of thing. But meanwhile, I at least got to start to see what I can do.

I will have to go to the embassy in Addis Ababa, but I don't want to do that yet because it means leaving Asmara, leaving the babies. The embassy has still been calling me from time to time just to make sure I'm okay.

Then I find out, all of a sudden, that the embassy is finally doing something. They are assigning someone independent to look into this. There is an American nun who teaches in the university in Asmara, Sister Dolores. Sister Dolores will be visiting with the family, and she will write a report for the embassy. God only knows what they are going to do with that report, I think. Probably nothing. I don't think there's much an American nun gonna do to help this situation, but at least something is happening.

I go back to cradling the sick babies, taking care of everyone. The very next day, as I'm changing one of the babies, Sister Dolores shows up. This nun is not your typical nun. She's not the quiet, soft-spoken type. This nun is a ball of fire, a take-charge person.

She and I love each other the second we meet. I know she's going to do everything in her power to help. I can tell by one look at her face, she is as shocked at twins' appearance as I am.

She takes in the whole situation, and I can see she is like me, nothing gets by her. She sees the family is starving, everyone sick. And right away she goes to work. She goes with me and the kids to a private doctor.

We sit in the waiting room together, each of us with a baby in our arms. One of the twins look so sick the people near us start edging away. I think they are afraid she gonna die right then and there.

Pretty soon we get called into the doctor's office. I tell him the whole story in a real rush. I tell him I'm trying to adopt them, I've got to document that they need to leave Asmara in order to survive.

"I need a paper saying they need to leave for their health," I tell him. Then I add, carefully, "It's got to say that they gonna die if they don't leave."

The doctor looks at me over his glasses, "That won't be a problem," he says.

It hits me in that second that that's what he thinks, too, that I might really lose them. Tears come up and I fight them down.

"I hope you understand what you are getting into. These are very sick babies. They have a bronchial infection, vitamin deficiencies, malnutrition. And this one," he looks in at Arsiema,and strokes her cheek gently, "This one, is going to, at the very least, need some surgery. She has some problems with her heart." Then he goes on, "Look, I can't make any promises, but in the meantime, while you are waiting here, I can prescribe some medicine and some special formula."

As he hands me the prescription, he says, "You know, I'm putting them on a pretty complicated schedule. They need to be fed frequently, they need different medicines."

I look him in the eye. "It's not a problem for me. I can do that."

I start to think about where I'm going to get these medicines since it doesn't seem like there is nothing to buy here, but he gives me some samples and tells me that with my prescription, I can get the rest.

I think a private doctor makes all the difference.

"I'll get started right away," I tell him.

He nods.

I'm happy to pay for the visit to the private doctor, and for the medicine.

He writes up a report about how the twins will die soon here. He tells how one has a heart condition, how they are malnourished, feverish, can hardly hold their heads up.

The nun don't waste no time. She just writes a report to send to the embassy. She tells them these kids are gonna die if they don't do something about it. She makes it sound ten times worse than I make it sound, and believe me, I make it sound bad enough.

"These kids are gonna die, if you don't let them leave," she writes. I know the embassy is thinking it is going to be a big embarrassment, 'specially since all the newspapers are in the act now.

Sister Dolores documents everything. She writes a big report on how they are sick, they have no energy, that Arsiema's tongue is hanging out and swollen, it's awful, it's an emergency. Temnit don't look too good, either. I don't know it, but the embassy is up to their necks in this situation. They are making frantic calls to INS. My congressman's office is making calls.

Meanwhile, I keep every paper in a file and I get all the documents together. I know I need to go back to the embassy, need to be there to make things happen. I been here, in Africa for a while now and my visa is only good for a little while longer. And I don't know if they'll renew it. I'm sure they all saying to themselves, "Can't wait to be rid of this lady."

So meantime, I show the twins' mother how to take care of the babies, give them their medicines and formula. I set everything up so I can leave Eritrea to go to the embassy in Addis Ababa. I hug the nun and make her promise to come by every day and check on the children. She hug me back. She got tears in her eyes. She really cares. She says, "Good luck, Ghabriela. May God take care of you."

I kiss the children, I say a prayer. I hope I'm gonna see them again alive. I'm not so sure.

I get on the plane and go to Addis Ababa, where the embassy is. I check into a boring hotel, no big communist brass here, but it's near the embassy. That's a good thing, because I plan on spending a lot of time there.

I call the people at the American embassy in Addis as soon as I get to the hotel. I can talk more freely now. I tell them I am alive, but I tell them, "These kids are going to die. You will have it on your conscience if these kids die here."

I talk to some official there who sounds like maybe he's someone important and I tell him how bad the kids look. I tell him how everyone back home is rooting for them, how people are writing letters.

He already knows most of this. Our embassy has been hearing from my congressman, from the nun, but I add to it, much as I can. I tell him, everyone is writing letters to the newspapers, to the Post, the Star, the New York papers.

"The whole world will know our embassy allowed these poor children to die for no reason. Everyone is interested in them. They more interested in them than they were even in the whales when the whole world watching. Besides," I say, trying to soften things, "I bet you are a good man. I bet you got children of your own, nieces, nephews. Do you want this on your conscience?"

I hear him sigh, "I wish there was something I could do. It's not like I want to single-handedly keep two starving babies here."

I can tell he's thinking like he doesn't really need this aggravation.

"Listen," he says, "You might try calling your congressman's office again. I know he's working on this, but another call can't hurt."

I take his hint. I call Congressman Solomon's office. I talk to the same man I talked to before I left.

He tells me how my story is showing up in the local papers every day. Everyone is following my progress. He tells me the office is getting letters, too, and they come from all over the country. "Congressman Solomon is doing everything he can, believe me," the assistant tells me. Then he says, "You know, he has a special place in his heart for adoption. It's not just all the publicity around this. He was adopted himself. He really wants this to happen for you."

This surprises me. But I file this information away in my head, because right now, I'm juggling a lot of things.

The next day, I go down to the embassy. I bring the file with me. Everyone at the embassy is so nice. I try hard to make friends with them and I do. I go there every day, and I ask after their families, their health. I connect with them. Other people are sitting in line, just sitting and waiting, but me, I've become family. They see me, they open the door, have me come in and get coffee.

I show them pictures of the twins, I tell them about them, I get them all involved. The women cluck over the pictures. "Poor little things. "Look how sick they look," they say.

I agree. I make friends with the highest guy at the embassy I can find. I show him the pictures, I give him the nun's report in person.

So far he hasn't seen the paperwork, he says. He has only heard the screaming nun.

I tell him how my congressman's office is working very hard. He knows the whole story by now. And he knows my congressman, Congressman Solomon. Everyone here knows and likes him. He's been here a lot on account of his being on the foreign relations committee. That doesn't hurt my case none, either.

I sigh and tell this man, "You know, it will be on your shoulder if they die." Meanwhile, poor guy got the nun calling him too, saying the same thing.

I'm getting pretty desperate, because my visa is almost running out. I call Wally one night, I'm so discouraged. It's not that easy to call, either, got to make arrangements, do this, do that, talk to this one, and it's very expensive. So we haven't talked very much, although he knows a little about what's going on.

But that night, I'm so upset I don't know what to do. I know time is running out and nothing is happening. I feel beaten down, like I'm done for. I can't bear to leave the kids here, either. Usually when this kind of stuff happens, I get angry, which probably works to my good. But somehow that night, the anger is gone, I'm just sad, defeated. I call Wally, sobbing.

"I don't know, Wally, if I can do it," I tell him. "The paperwork isn't coming through, no one is moving fast enough, nothing is happening. The kids are gonna die because of the red tape, and I can't do anything. It's not right."

Wally talks softly to me, tells me to just do my best. He says it's in God's hands. Nothing more I can do. He tells me the story is still in the newspapers, that they are still following my progress. He sighs and says he saw an article just this morning saying, "Washington Still Says No to Twins." Then he adds, "Listen, Ghabriela, don't do anything rash."

I know there is no point telling him about all my thoughts about running away with the kids. It will just give him an upset stomach and rash. I just tell him goodnight, I love him, and I'll be home soon. I keep all my crazy thoughts to myself. I lie in bed that night, tears running down my cheeks.

The next day, it's hard to get out of bed and face the routine at the embassy again, but I do. I get dressed, put on my make-up, bring my documents. I'm planning on saying "Goodbye" to everyone. But as soon as I open the door, instead of hearing the usual "Hi, Ghabriela, help yourself to some coffee," everyone runs to me, hugging, screaming, yelling all at once. "Congratulations," they say. "We got the INS approval this morning."

I'm shocked. I scream, too, jump up and down, thank God, hug everyone near me. "What happened, how did they do it?" I ask.

"They are letting them in for humanitarian reasons. Your congressman got a special permission from Congress just for them."

They didn't change the law. I'm disappointed about that, but this is no time to think of that. I am just thrilled I can bring them home. I say a special prayer for my congressman.

I got lots to do. I got paperwork to do for the twins, and I got to get them here from Eritrea. I can't go back to Eritrea, so getting them here isn't going to be that easy. But you know me, I'm an arranger. I start making plans.

I will have to get the mom to bring the twins. She has never been on an airplane before, and she isn't in such good shape to begin with. But I got one thing going in my favor. She is motivated. She wants the twins to live, to go to America and she wants to please me. And I can work through the nun, get her to help me.

I buy airplane tickets for the mom and the twins. I tell the nun everything she must do. It's really important they get to the airport, by noon tomorrow.

In the meantime, I try to buy some clothes for the trip, some food for the babies. I can't find regular diapers so I got to buy paper diapers. Can you believe that thirty paper diapers and two pairs of cheaply made shoes run me about fifty American dollars? That's more than the average family makes altogether in one month in Ethiopia. I don't know where all those babies in Ethiopia gonna be doing their business, but it surely isn't in regulation type diapers. My guess is people use rags when they can find them, although I bet there isn't too much extra stuff to make rags out of.

The next day, I meet the mom and twins at the plane. The mom looks terrible. She's been sick anyway and there is some delay, the plane's been sitting on runway for hours or circling, something, and she's been sitting with sick kids and no diapers.

The kids look awful and smell worse. I bring them right down to the embassy. I want everyone there to know how desperate the situation is. I want all the paperwork to get done fast and go through.

When we get to the embassy, they won't let the mother in. She's Eritrean and she was cradling two very dirty smelly kids and they don't want her near the place. But they know me, and besides, I'm an American citizen; they have to let me in. I take the babies from the mother's arms and carry them in but I don't clean them up or nothing.

Well, you should see the commotion. The people in the embassy have been following my story for weeks now. They all want to help. They find a place to wash the kids, someone goes to the neighbors to get clothes, food everything. Someone rips up her bed sheets to make strips of cloth for diapers. Everyone gets into the act. They bathe the kids, clean them up, put fresh stuff on them.

Years later, when I send the embassy pictures, the people there told me they thought for sure on that day that at least one of the kids would die.

And they get all the paperwork done in a hurry. Fastest packet of immigration papers ever done, I bet. I'm cleared with the U.S. INS. The people at the airline arrange tickets for me fast to get on the plane. They have told all the flight attendants about us, too. Everyone is involved.

Finally, I get on the plane with the babies. The people I've made friends with from the embassy come with me, wave goodbye to me and the girls. People are cheering. It's a regular three- ring circus. Even the airline people are involved. When I get on the plane, I find we got a row of seats to ourselves. The flight attendants have set it up that way to give us some room. They are cooing over the babies. Although, to tell you the truth, when they look in at Arsiema and see how sick she looks, I think they are a little shocked, but they got to cover it up and put on that "Oh, aren't the babies cute" voice with all the cooing and stuff. But no matter, the flight attendants try to help out. They hold the babies, they help me feed them, they find something I can set them down to sleep in.

The babies are so sick, they just sleep.

And me, I been working on pure adrenaline for days now. All of a sudden, all that adrenaline is gone, and I'm completely exhausted. I don't think about anything. I don't think about what I'm gonna have to worry about medically, whether they'll survive, how I'll raise them — nothing. I just know I'm going home with my babies.

I settle into sleep. But then, sometime in the middle of the flight, after a couple hours sleep, I wake up. Everything around me is quiet, the window shades are drawn, the other passengers are mostly sleeping, too, because it's night out. And I look down at the babies next to me and it hits me at once. It's the first time in my life someone really needs me. And I got the family I been dreaming about since the time I was a little girl. I got the husband, the kids. I don't think about what happens next, I just fall asleep.

CHAPTER

18

My plane lands at the airport in New York City, which is about a three hours' drive from where we live. Wally will be there, but we've been told by the embassy not to tell anyone I'm coming. The embassy told me to just go, get out of the country with the babies as quietly as I can, no newspapers, no nothing. So when I land at the airport it is quiet, and just Wally is there. I can tell he's relieved I'm back and I'm safe. He looks down at the girls and I know something inside him change in that minute. For the first time in his life, he's a father.

We drive up to Saratoga that night, and the twins are so sick and tired they just sleep all the way in the car. I'm too revved up to sleep. I feel like I had eighteen cups of coffee, feel that jittery- can't- settle -down feeling. I can hardly sit still for the car ride.

Thank God Wally's arranged to take two weeks off from work to stay home and help me. At first, when he tells me, I think, now why does he need to go do that? I think I won't need help. I figure I can take care of a couple of babies with no problem. I don't think about all the emotions gonna come at me, about how tired I'm gonna be. I just spent weeks seeing people starving to death, seeing war, famine. And too, being there in Asmara was bringing up lots of old memories for me, some that were better off staying way down buried under a lot of other stuff, believe me. But now those old memories pop up, that old anger popping up too. And on top of that, I'm so excited I just got my life dream to come true. Tell you the truth, I don't know what to feel. I think I'm so exhausted, for right then, I don't feel nothing except glad to be home and have Wally take care of things for a little while.

And I'm glad to see he brought a huge bag of stuff, all the stuff I tell him. He got real diapers and real baby food. In Asmara, if any kids want to eat solid food, they better like spice. And he also brought clothes and coats, bless his soul. When we get home I find Wally's got the refrigerator stocked with milk, juice, baby food, everything we'll need. We got a room all set up for the twins and I try to feed them some baby food that night, but they are too tired to eat. I give them bottles of formula and we all collapse into bed.

The next day I wake up and I see people on my lawn. I can hardly believe it. There are reporters wandering around with cameras. Somehow they got wind of the story. I'm still in shock about this, when Wally shows me the newspaper headlines. They say things like "Couple Wins Battle to Save Twins," "Permission to Bring Back Twins Granted," and "She's Back and She's Got the Twins!"

I smile. I can't believe we actually did it.

But right then, I got more important things to think about. I got babies to feed, bottles to warm, medicine to mix. And I'm trying to figure out basic things, like how to get the twins to let me go for a second. If I get up to leave the room, they scream.

Naptime is also a struggle. I try putting them down for a nap but they want me to stay with them, lay down next to them. I do and we all lie down in the bed together, but each twin wants me to face her, but I only got one face. Suddenly I'm feeling needed, loved, like I really got a purpose. At first I'm just a whirlwind of activity. I don't have much chance to think.

But then, a few days later, I finally get a chance to sit quietly. The babies are both sleeping, and Wally is out doing errands. The sun is shining in, warming a spot on the couch. All the excitement of actually getting the babies is starting to quiet down. I begin to think more about what's really happened. I look down and see my two little girls, and know my life is totally changed. All of a sudden everything from the time in Asmara comes rushing at me. I start to think about my old life, how lucky I was to get away when I did. And I think how nice I'm gonna make their lives. I want to make their lives perfect. I don't want them to feel about me the way I feel about my sister, 'bout all those people who just let me suffer. I remember Andu's words about thinking about how you want people to remember you. I know in this minute I would do anything in the world for them.

I peek in their carriage, look at them sleeping under their blanket. They look so little. They are still breathing hard, got a little bronchitis left. I put my hands on their chests, feel them moving up and down. But I don't care how sick they are, I am going to make them live. I coax them as they sleep, give them a pep talk about the great life I'm gonna give them, but, I tell them, they got to do their part and pull through.

I even have a conversation with God about this. I tell Him, "Look, you know, you took my first baby, my baby boy. I sure never did understand it, and just between you and me, I didn't think it was very fair. But did I give up? No, I did not. Did I trash everything, turn on you? No, I did not. I kept right on going to church, right on trying my best to live a good life. All right, there's that part about selling myself and all, but it wasn't like you gave me any great choices. Let's see, should I be a rich lady who goes out every night to charity balls or should I go to the bar and sell myself? I want to eat. I do what I got to do. To tell you the truth, I always think you understand about that and don't hold it against me none. And I make something of my life, I do something good for someone else. So now it's your turn. You got to work with me here."

I say all this as I'm sitting near the babies, watching over them. Of course, the priests would probably gasp if they knew what I say, but it's what I feel.

After I have this little talk with God, I fall asleep. I sleep right there on the couch, and I have a dream, a dream that my mother comes to me and visits. Well, of course my mother has a history of showing up in people's dreams. Same mother famous for showing up in my sister's dreams, couldn't rest until she sees my sister put me somewhere safe. This time my mother comes to me in a dream. She smiles at me, and tells me she is happy for me, and with me.

I feel warm, peaceful in that dream. But then I tell her I'm worried about the twins, worried God will steal them from me. Sure, they been looking better and better, plumping out some, but that don't guarantee me nothing. I couldn't bear to lose another child, I tell her.

My mother smiles, tells me everything is going to be okay. I see her starting to fade, and I yank her back. You know, it's kind of funny all the bad times I been through, wasn't like I talked to my mother all the times in my dreams. She must have been saving this visit for something really important.

When I yank her back, I say I got another fear, a fear no one understands. I tell her I'm afraid I'm not going to be the kind of mother I want to be. I don't know nothing about raising kids. All my time as a kid, people were beating me, yelling at me. Never had a mother to teach me how to be a good mother.

She pauses for a minute. "You got a good heart, Ghabriela. You'll figure out what you need to do," she tells me, "Remember that." And then she goes.

I think about that for a while. It comforts me. I don't know what lies ahead for me and my girls, but I know I've got my dream, and I'm gonna do my best. And after that day, I feel in my heart, that it is all going to work out, that I'm going to make it, and the kids are going to make it.

Ghabriela's Epilogue:

So that's my story. Telling my story got me to think differently about my life and the people in it and all the things that happened to me. I understand that all those things made me who I am. And all those things fit together somehow, they are a part of something bigger. Sometimes, I still feel anger, anger toward the people who mistreated me as a child. But along the way, I came to understand that anger don't do me any good, don't do nobody any good. I can't get rid of it and sometimes it still come up, sometimes still cause me problems, but I try turning my anger a different way. I try to use it to do some good. I start to look around for things to do to help people. I help people in my neighborhood; I do what I can.

Now my girls are all grown up and have children of their own. Oh, we had all the usual problems, but they both turned out pretty good. They graduated from college, one of them went to graduate school, become a teacher. Can't tell you how proud that made me, especially considering I didn't have much school myself.

Wally passed away a couple of years ago. I stayed married to Wally for a lot of years, but somehow over time we just grow apart. Even though we got divorced, and we had some bad times in the beginning, we mended things over the years. I know Wally did a lot of good of things for me, and I don't forget that, even if he made me crazy sometimes. My daughters think sometime he was the guardian angel of us all and I feel that way too.

At first I wanted to tell my story for my kids. They were in their teens when I first thought about this. When I bring the twins home when they were infants, I think they are gonna grow up and are going to adore me, appreciate me every second for saving their lives, realize what they didn't have to go through. But no, it wasn't like that, not at all because of course, they don't know nothing except the life they live. They think their biggest problems are what boy to go out with, how to talk their mother into letting them stay out later, give them the car keys, whatever. They worry about the right jeans, the right sneakers, the right hair. They did all the things regular kids did, went to high school and graduated, followed all the fashions, listened to hip hop and rap, got themselves boyfriends, although to tell you the truth, their boyfriends didn't always thrill me none. But still, in my own heart, I know what I saved them from and for me, that is an important part of my story.

There is a fable I heard about an old man at the beach tossing starfish back into the ocean. The story tells of thousands of starfish lying on the sand, just washed in by the tide. Those starfish can't do nothing, they are just left on the beach to dry up and die. An old man begins to toss a starfish back in the ocean. Just then, a young man comes along and asks, "Old man, why do you toss that starfish back when there are so many thousands lying here? What difference can it possibly make?" The man looks at the starfish in his hand and says, "To this starfish it makes all the difference," and tosses it back.

I understand this story. This story run through my life. Sometimes, I been that starfish, and sometimes I been the old man. It work both ways.

I want all the people in my life who have helped me to know how much I appreciated them. I especially want Congressman Gerald Solomon's family to know how much he did for me and my family. There were many other people who offered kindness, although the person that shaped my life the most may have been my brother. To all those people along the way, I offer thanks. And I want to thank Betty Gallagher and Ellie Parker for getting my story out there.

Author's Afterword

When I started to meet with Ghabriela, I knew I wanted to tell her story, although I wasn't sure exactly why at first. But as I began to hear more and more or it, I realized that there was a universality about her story, about suffering and dislocations, that could be understood in broader terms.

In writing this story, I thought about how and why Ghabriela was so resilient. It seemed to me that some of her resilience was with her from birth. She was optimistic, she dreamt big, she never gave up, and she was sure of herself. Despite the fact that she suffered through hunger, neglect, and abuse, Ghabriela always reached out to others and understood that every kindness makes a difference. But I think that just as important as her disposition, was the fact that along the way there were people who made a real difference in her life. There were people who changed her thinking about the world, and about herself. Her brother, in particular, showed kindness and empathy that made a deep impression on her.

During the time I was writing this, I heard about the concept of restorative narrative. The term captured the idea that telling the stories of people who had experienced trauma but had been able to rebuild their lives, could be empowering for everyone, and could help us understand resilience. In telling this story I came to realize how much small gestures and kindnesses can mean to people in the midst of trauma. And even in what seems to be a hopeless situation, throwing back the starfish remains important!

ACKNOWLEDGEMENTS

I am indebted to Ghabriela for telling me her story and to Betty Gallagher for introducing us and encouraging me to write this story.

I want to thank the many people who read this over and over and made insightful suggestions. These include Robin Eichen, Marsha Rosenblum, Sally Harder, Betty Gallagher, Nancy Butcher Ohlin, Nancy Seid, Matt Witten, Barbara Ann Porte and Carolyn Porte Lieberman. I especially want to thank Nancy Seid and John DeDakis for editing the book for me. I also want to thank the many people who supported me emotionally through this including my family and people from the Creative Bloc. Countless other people helped me in numerous ways with this project.

Ghabriela wishes to thank the many people who helped her along the way, especially those who helped her in adopting her children. These include Congressman Gerald Solomon and all the children who wrote letters and the journalists who kept the story going.

CPSIA information can be obtained
at www.ICGtesting.com
Printed in the USA
BVOW11s0532060417
480384BV00001B/71/P